A TRAUMA-INFORMED
APPROACH TO LIBRARY SERVICES

A TRAUMA-INFORMED APPROACH TO LIBRARY SERVICES

REBECCA TOLLEY

ALA
Editions

CHICAGO   2020

Rebecca Tolley is a professor and librarian at East Tennessee State University. She coordinates the Sherrod Library's research consultation service. She speaks and publishes on topics such as organizational culture, customer services in libraries, and cultivating empathy in librarians and library workers. She coedited *Generation X Librarian: Essays on Leadership, Technology, Pop Culture, Social Responsibility and Professional Identity* (2011) and *Mentoring in Librarianship: Essays on Working with Adults and Students to Further the Profession* (2011). Her writing has appeared in anthologies, several library journals, and numerous reference works.

Extensive effort has gone into ensuring the reliability of the information in this book; however, the publisher makes no warranty, express or implied, with respect to the material contained herein.

ISBN: 978-0-8389-1981-1 (paper)

Library of Congress Cataloging-in-Publication Data

Names: Tolley, Rebecca, 1971- author.
Title: A trauma-informed approach to library services / Rebecca Tolley.
Description: Chicago : ALA Editions, 2020. | Includes bibliographical references and index. |
    Summary: "This book applies a trauma-informed care framework to library services.
    This approach can foster empathetic service, positive patron encounters, and a trusting
    workplace"—Provided by publisher.
Identifiers: LCCN 2020009880 | ISBN 9780838919811 (paperback)
Subjects: LCSH: Libraries and people with social disabilities—United States. | Library outreach
    programs—United States. | Psychic trauma.
Classification: LCC Z711.92.S6 T65 2020 | DDC 027.6/63—dc23
LC record available at https://lccn.loc.gov/2020009880

Cover design by Alejandra Diaz. Images © New Africa (top left); Chanintorn.V (top right); Stanislav (bottom).

Text design in the Chaparral, Gotham, and Bell Gothic typefaces.

♾ This paper meets the requirements of ANSI/NISO Z39.48-1992 (Permanence of Paper).

Printed in the United States of America

24 23 22 21 20   5 4 3 2 1

Contents

Preface

The idea for this project began as an article and then expanded into a book. I've always found inspiration for new library customer service models from outside the profession and have thought about ways to adapt them to our operations. New approaches to customer service in libraries, and in all service industries, are popular and needed because they identify new practices and help us develop systems that serve our library patrons where they are. When I say "where they are," I mean at the point of need, but I also mean where patrons are personally and at what level they are comfortable accepting our help. Some libraries excel at customer service, while others fail. There are various reasons for this. It may be an individual library staff problem, or it may be due to the operational or organizational climate. A trauma-informed framework can help us build empathy for those whom we serve at the individual staff level, as well as investing empathy within our operations and throughout the organization.

In the last few years, graduate and undergraduate students with whom I've worked have exposed me to trauma theory, mostly in their need for articles to support papers and assignments in nursing. Over the course of the last two or three years those requests for help expanded from students and faculty in psychology, and then in social work, education, and public health. Many of those research requests came from students working with faculty in those departments because East Tennessee State University's (ETSU) faculty are well-grounded in adverse childhood experiences (ACEs) and trauma-informed care (TIC). As a member of our Women's Studies Program's Steering Committee, I was asked to moderate a panel on feminist pedagogy at the Southeastern Women's Studies Association's annual conference at Clemson University in 2018. While there, the department's administrative assistant posed questions to participants on independent panels about whether or how their work was trauma informed. She and the program director for ETSU's Women's Studies program wanted to bring trauma-informed practices to a higher education setting where we serve a population of students who have experienced childhood trauma. They invited me and other Steering Committee members to the Highlander Research Center in New Market, Tennessee, for a summer retreat, "Trauma-Informed Care & Changing the Narrative of Gender-Based Violence on Campus and in the WMST Classroom," where one of our social work faculty members educated everyone about ACEs and trauma-informed philosophies.

From then on, my awareness of childhood trauma, ACEs, and resilience skyrocketed. I read scholarly articles and popular books. I watched TED Talks. I attended more trauma-informed care workshops, self-care workshops, and the like until I was saturated in the topic's philosophy and practices.

Naturally, I wondered how effective a trauma-informed approach might be for making improvements to customer service in libraries. An awareness of ACEs and childhood trauma increased my empathy for everyone I help in the library, and frankly, all of humanity. It is my hope that sharing information about this framework with library staff can increase their compassion and responsiveness in the areas of customer service. But trauma-informed care also holds promise for organizational transformation, as well. In fact, an objective of trauma-informed care moves beyond awareness and education and into organizational systems and transmitting the framework via institutional policies, practices, and procedures.

While every library may not be ready for these changes at the organizational level, an awareness of trauma-informed care by individuals can help nudge libraries in that direction. Wanting to change and improve our libraries' customer services is an ongoing objective. Transforming that urge and passion into action can be difficult, however. This book will give library staff ideas for small ways they can change their thinking, as well as ways to change their personal practices of librarianship and customer service in pursuit of these goals. Change can come from above, from the middle, or from below. A commitment to small but meaningful personal changes can pay off in large ways. However, for sustainable and universal adoption of the TIC framework, leadership must buy in. Therefore, this book is for both individuals and organizations.

In part I of this book I will explain psychological trauma and adverse childhood experiences, trauma-informed approaches to services, trauma-informed care and libraries, and the trauma-informed built environment. In part II I will address the six key principles of trauma-informed care: safety; transparency and trustworthiness; peer support; collaboration and mutuality; empowerment, voice, and choice; and cultural, historical, and gender issues. In part III I will discuss assessing organizational readiness, the library as sanctuary, building a trauma-informed library workforce, long-term planning for trauma-informed services, and short-term solutions for trauma-informed services.

Please note that some people are very opposed to identifying anything psychological as *trauma*. Some professionals and scholars only recognize trauma as experienced in war zones. They don't recognize that domestic and family violence can create as much or more post-traumatic stress disorder (PTSD) in survivors as wartime experiences can. Likewise, some institutions are careful with their language. Rather than use *trauma*, Harvard University's Center on the Developing Child uses the term *toxic stress* to identify the same dynamic. Still other institutions and authorities use the term *traumatic stress*. But all three of these concepts are synonymous. And all three of them use adverse childhood experiences as a baseline for understanding the dynamic, explain the same neurobiological adaptations the brain and body make to childhood trauma, and discuss the same interventions that lead to resilience and positive lifelong outcomes.

Acknowledgments

I hope that readers find value in this book. The work of Monte-Angel Richardson, Danica San Juan, Bryce Kozla, Dr. Meghan Harper, Sasha Conley, Aaron Ferguson, Alana Kumbier, Michelle Gohr, Vitaline A Nova, and Karina Hagelin add much to our understanding of trauma-informed and trauma-responsive practices in libraries of all types.

I'm most grateful to Patrick Hogan, Senior Editor at ALA Editions, who read my query and liked it enough of it to bring it before the editorial team at ALA Editions, who then gave a thumbs up to publishing it. He read chapters out of order as I sent them to him and responded with thoughtful comments about organization, structure, and tone. Thank you to Paul Mendelson and Samantha Imburgia who edited my work; made line edits, changes, and suggestions that enhanced my writing; and helped me keep my facts straight. Thanks to Jill Hillemeyer and Robert Christopher for their marketing efforts. Much appreciation to Alejandra Diaz for the cover design, as it exceeded my expectations. I thank Lauren Ehle who laid out the manuscript and worked on the interior. Thank you to Angela Gwizdala who reviewed the manuscript and approved the interior layout and cover design. Everyone at ALA Editions was professional, responsive, and easy to work with. I'm especially grateful for their efforts at producing my work, and the work of other authors at ALA Editions, during an extraordinary time in the first half of 2020 when we all added the stress and anxiety of the coronavirus pandemic to our full lives.

The following people are a mixture of those whom I know in real life and those whose conference presentations or books and articles aided my understanding of trauma-informed care and adverse childhood experiences: Dr. Julia Bernard, Dr. Andi Clements, Dr. Stephanie Covington, Dr. Dottie Saxon Greene, Becky Haas, Dr. Nadine Burke Harris, Cindi Olson Huss, Deanna Irick, Dr. Judy McCook, Gabor Maté, Liz Murray, Donna Jackson Nakazawa, Leah Lakshmi Piepzna-Samarasinha, Dr. Megan Quinn, Nancy Roark, Terri Sloan, Sonya Renee Taylor, Dr. Bessel van der Kolk, Mark Wolynn, and Dr. Meira Yasin.

My dear teachers and professors have shaped my thinking and writing and to them I owe many thanks: Henry Joy, Dr. Charles Griffith, Callie Redd, Gwendolyn Wash, Judy Odom, Carol Transou, Laura Waddey, Lynn Whitehead, Jack Schrader, Dr. Ray Salvatore Jennings, Dr. Martha Copp, Dr. James V. Carmichael, Dr. Doug Burgess, Dr. Elwood Watson, and Tayari Jones.

I'm grateful for the friendship and support of several colleagues, including Ross Bowron, Magda Underdown-DuBois, Alison Lampley, Evan Schmoll, and Sarah Maeve Whisnant. I thank faculty and staff at Sherrod Library whose work provided the interlibrary loans and purchases for my research: Myra Smith, Jennifer Young, and Brooke Garland. I thank Joanna Anderson whose commiseration, joyful energy, and singing from her office I miss each day. I thank Dr. Phyllis Thompson whose kindness, grace, empathy, and hospitality know no bounds. I thank Dr. Jamie Branam Brown for her warmth and grace. I thank Dr. Wendy Doucette whose encouragement, kind words, and wise counsel keep me somewhat sane. She is an amazing collaborator whose knack for writing structure, knowledge of legal ethics, and culling of extraneous wording is peerless.

I thank friends Carol Patrick, Laura Mullins Tomlinson, Debbie DiBona, Scout Taylor, Keaira Ware, Melissa Curran, and Vaughn Teegarden whose loving hearts, caring, and advice I could not live without.

A lifetime of thanks to my parents Debra Miller and Larry Tolley whose love supports me. I thank my favorite, and only, sister Jessica Hoffman for her careful listening to and bolstering of me, and for loving this book's cover as much as I do.

Most of all, I am grateful for my daughter Elsa, whose daily presence in my life makes it complete. She compels me to become a better person. Her and every child's future drives me toward improving the world in which we live for everyone. She asked how the book was going as I wrote the bulk of it and pointed out all the times our cat Wendy sat on the printed manuscript pages to "help" during the last edits.

PART I

Adverse Childhood Experiences and Trauma-Informed Care

1

Trauma and Adverse Childhood Experiences

When we think about psychological trauma, many of us default to thinking about overt, external examples, like the emotional trauma suffered by war veterans or the survivors of natural disasters. And it is true that trauma was traditionally classified as resulting from events outside the range of normal human experience. But Mark Epstein (2013) reminds us that trauma isn't just what happens after Hurricane Katrina, school shootings at Virginia Tech, or a terrorist incident. Trauma happens to everyone. He says that the undercurrent of trauma informs ordinary life.

WHAT IS TRAUMA?

So what exactly do we mean by the term *psychological trauma*, or simply *trauma* (as it is now often referred to)? Psychological trauma is damage or injury to the psyche that results from an extremely frightening or distressing event or experience. These events and experiences usually involve a threat to our psychological or physical well-being. Trauma can result from a single painful event, a prolonged event, recurring events, or a series of ongoing, relentless stresses. The trauma typically occurs due to an overwhelming amount of stress that exceeds a person's ability to cope or to integrate the painful emotions involved.

Life-threatening events like combat or natural disasters have traditionally been associated with trauma, and particularly with PTSD, but trauma resulting from childhood abuse or neglect, domestic violence, or rape is far more common in the population and occurs on a larger scale. Children are especially susceptible to emotional trauma because they are generally more vulnerable and lack the coping skills and capacities of adults. Traumas sustained during childhood are known as *adverse childhood experiences* or ACEs.

A trauma survivor, especially those whose traumas date from childhood, may not be able to remember what actually happened to them because the painful emotions they experienced at the time have been buried in the unconscious, a phenomenon known as repressed memory, or *repression*. These repressed memories can cause various mental disorders later in life that involve anxiety, depression, dissociation, or other syndromes. The recommended treatment for these mental disorders is some type of therapy. More broadly, any psychic damage done to the individual early in life can have serious, negative consequences over the long term.

After a traumatic experience, a person may reexperience the trauma mentally due to trigger reminders, or *triggers*. This phenomenon is also known as *re-traumatization*. The flashbacks, panic attacks, and nightmares that afflict combat veterans and other PTSD patients are the best-known examples of this tendency to relive or reexperience a traumatic event from the past.

ADVERSE CHILDHOOD EXPERIENCES

It is important to note that the definitions of *trauma*, and of the *adverse childhood experiences* that are its chief cause, have continued to broaden in recent years. A landmark study on ACEs conducted by Kaiser-Permanente from 1995 to 1997 studied over 17,000 patients receiving health care from the organization. The results of the data collected indicated that nearly two-thirds of study participants reported at least one ACE, and more than one in five reported three or more ACEs. Surprisingly, a majority of this population was white and middle-class. The Centers for Disease Control and Prevention (CDC) website offers much information on adverse childhood experiences, including findings from this study (www.cdc.gov/violenceprevention/childabuseandneglect/acestudy). Figure 1.1 is derived from an infographic on the CDC website and shows demographic information from the ACE study.

Given our cultural biases, researchers and laypersons assume and expect ACEs in communities of color and poor populations. Since the ACE study's data disproved our ideas about trauma's prevalence within the underclass, policymakers ignored its findings for many years because of what it revealed about American families and the universality of childhood experiences. The

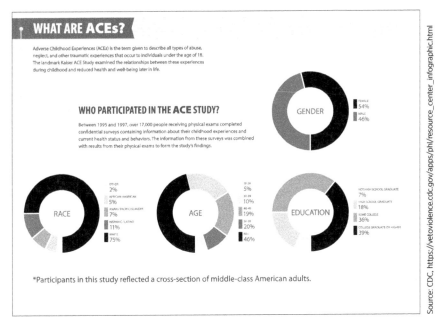

Source: CDC, https://vetoviolence.cdc.gov/apps/phi/resource_center_infographic.html

FIGURE 1.1

What Are ACEs?

results hit too close to home; the truth is that nearly everyone experiences adverse childhood trauma. It crosses socioeconomic classes, ethnicities, race, religious beliefs, geographical regions, and all the other demographic markers.

Categorized by incidents of abuse, neglect, and family dysfunction, ACEs include situations or events happening prior to the person's eighteenth birthday that extend beyond the normal challenges of growing to adulthood that everyone experiences. The period of time between childhood and adulthood has lengthened over the years, in part due to elementary and secondary education requirements, as well as child labor laws and changes to American parenting philosophies that infantilize people well into their third decade. The lengthening life span of Americans has also expanded the time given to children, adolescents, and young adults to navigate developmental tasks as they try on different identities. This is a typical part of exploring careers and lifestyles before settling into long-term goals for adulthood.

The developing brain is affected by chronic, or toxic, stress. The brain's response to stressful events heightens, and when its stress response is on constant high alert, this results in long-term inflammation and disease, but more importantly, it leaves the adult with a high ACEs score, which makes them more likely to overreact to everyday stressors like heavy traffic, waiting in long queues, or not finding a parking space at work; occasions that many adults easily navigate. When a person's baseline is this high, the smallest incident may trigger a negative feedback loop from which escape is difficult without deep reflection and the use of healing modalities. Chronic stress also ages the child on a cellular level, eroding their telomeres as well, thus setting them up for early debilitating disease. The more the brain is stressed in childhood, the more the hippocampus shrinks. The hippocampus is responsible for processing emotion and memory and managing stress. Between the brain's high stress setting and the hippocampus's dwindling size, it's easy to understand how children feel chronic anxiety and its long-term physiological effects.

Children with high ACEs scores who lack loving adults in their lives transition into adolescence with poor decision-making skills and executive functions and are more likely to develop mood disorders that involve anxiety or depression. This pattern continues into adulthood, leaving adults with high ACE scores easily stressed and overreactive in most situations, unless they've encountered and incorporated coping skills like therapy, meditation, mindfulness, yoga, immersion in nature, acupuncture, and other brain-body approaches.

When children experience one or more of ten types of traumatic incidents recognized by the ACEs study instrument, the resulting stress can impair their coping skills for the challenges of everyday life, and can even increase their risk factors for chronic, debilitating disease. The most commonly occurring of these ten types of experiences are child abuse, household challenges (chiefly domestic violence), and child neglect. Within these categories, childhood experiences are divided further.

ABUSE

Abuse includes emotional, physical, and sexual abuse. Emotional abuse may involve an attempt to control another person, and often the adult is unaware that their behavior is abusive, as they've adopted their parenting or relational techniques from their own dysfunctional parents or family. The behavior includes accusations, blaming, and monitoring of the child's activities and behaviors. Emotionally abusive parents constantly criticize their child's talking, dressing, communications with others, and coping mechanisms, using this criticism as a form of control. These parents use sarcasm, name-calling, and verbal assaults to dominate children. Emotionally abusive parents withhold affection as punishment, refuse to communicate with the child at all, and isolate the child from family and friends who support them. Finally, they refuse to acknowledge their part in the family dynamic and rarely take responsibility for their actions or apologize. Physical abuse happens when a parent or caregiver inflicts a physical injury on the child or adolescent's body. These injuries can be marks, cuts, bruises, welts, muscle sprains, broken or burnt skin, broken bones, and other bodily indicators.

The survivors of child abuse don't trust authority figures, for many reasons. Even though they may not recognize parental negligence or abuse, experiencing it affects a child's ability to trust anyone. They have learned that authority is punitive and takes things away. "Authority figures" in the form of law enforcement officers and social workers acting on behalf of the state remove children from their parents when there's an altercation or a report of abuse or neglect. The bank or creditors take belongings away from homes when parents default on loans, thus leaving their parents afraid, anxious, and angry. Trauma survivors have zero positive interactions with authority. The model they have observed vis-à-vis their parent's interactions has left them with the belief that authority takes and punishes, but never gives or soothes.

The survivors of child abuse sometimes become aggressive or display other behavioral problems. Usually they suffer high anxiety and are always on the alert, reading the signs for when the parent or caregiver is likely to strike out at them again. Abused children often suffer post-traumatic stress disorder (PTSD) and allied emotional reactions. Children growing up in physically abusive environments become hypervigilant to anger so that they can quickly identify and absent themselves from the violent parent.

Children who are sexually abused experience unwanted sexual activity with adults or older children who use force, make threats, and otherwise take advantage of them. Some child sexual trauma survivors experience disassociation, which deals with memory. The memory of the abuse is not lost, but its recovery is impossible or spotty. Thus, children, adolescents, and adults with these experiences exhibit memory disturbances, which may affect them in many situations, including studying, reading, knowledge-building, and information-seeking. The survivors of child abuse also experience low self-esteem. Children who survive emotional, physical, or sexual abuse internalize their injuries and deploy self-criticism because they believe that something is inherently wrong with them and they asked for or deserved the abuse. People may believe that physical abuse is worse than emotional abuse, but the brain regions relaying information about emotional pain and physical pain are the same; emotional abuse is experienced at the same level as physical pain by our nervous system.

HOUSEHOLD CHALLENGES

Household challenges include situations in which the child's mother was treated violently, or in which any of the following occurred in the family: substance abuse, mental illness, separation and/or divorce, or incarceration of a household member. Domestic violence, or intimate partner violence (IPV), reflects destructive patterns of behaviors in which one partner maintains power and control over another. This dynamic involves physical or sexual violence, threats and intimidation, emotional abuse, and economic dispossession. Children easily become pawns in the IPV pattern. Figure 1.2 shows how at the center of physical and sexual violence in a household there is a need for power and control. Power when used and manipulated in this fashion affects children's self-esteem and can cause anxiety, depression, and, in extreme cases, PTSD. Children believe that what they experience within the family is normal. Without exposure to healthy family models, children who are manipulated and coerced may likely continue these patterns in their intimate relationships and families when they become adults.

Tobacco, alcohol, and both prescription and illegal drugs are substances that parents and caregivers abuse within a family setting. Prenatal exposure to these substances can greatly affect children and is associated with miscarriage, stillbirth, and sudden infant death syndrome. Exposure may cause low birth weight and physical deformities, cognitive impairment, conduct disorders, depression, or mental retardation. Furthermore, substance abuse within the family can lead to IPV, divorce, exposure to crime, and poverty. Children's experience of substance abuse within their family may predispose them to abuse substances as adolescents and adults.

Source: Domestic Abuse Intervention Programs (www.theduluthmodel.org)

FIGURE 1.2
Power and Control Wheel

Likewise, when a parent or caregiver experiences mental illness, it affects children and their development. A parent with untreated bipolar disorder cannot recognize how their disease affects their children as it seeps into their behavior and takes root in their psychology. Mental illness can affect a person's ability to parent and may create impaired parenting and family discord. Untreated mental illness is strongly associated with general family dissonance, marital problems, and a chaotic home environment, all of which can damage childhood emotional development. Children thrive in safe, stable environments and rely, for the most part, on the parent behaving dependably and creating an atmosphere of calm and security. According to the National Alliance on Mental Illness, one in five adults (43.8 million, or 18.5 percent) in the United States experiences mental illness each year. Their data reveals that 1.1 percent of adults live with schizophrenia, 2.6 percent live with bipolar disorder, 4 percent have experienced PTSD, 6.9 percent have had a major depressive episode, and 18.1 percent have experienced any of various anxiety disorders.

Researchers identify the aforementioned mental illnesses as *serious mental illnesses* (SMI). Children with SMI parents have a child psychiatric diagnosis of 30 to 50 percent. Children growing up in homes affected by mental illness feel lonely, vulnerable, helpless, and invisible. They experience their family environment as terrifying and impossible to adjust to. Information about their parents' mental illness may be withheld or considered shameful, which fuels their stress and anxiety. Children with mentally ill parents sometimes become the caregiver, are "parentified," and are robbed of the carefree atmosphere that childhood should provide within families. Moreover, when all of the family's focus and resources are spent on the mentally ill adult, the children's needs can be overlooked or dismissed. Untreated mental illness affects children in that they display impaired social functioning, exhibit poor academic performance, experience mood disturbances, and have poor emotional regulation. They experience anger, anxiety, and guilt while also feeling socially isolated due to shame and stigma. Their risk of drug use and poor social relationships increases.

Dissolution of the family unit due to parental separation, estrangement, or divorce can have long-term effects on children's psychology and make it more difficult for them to form healthy attachments in adulthood. These events also tend to introduce great financial change in children's lives. Generally a divorce increases a child's dependence on their parents and other family members and caregivers, but it works in the opposite way with adolescents: it accelerates their independence. Learning to transition between one or more households with different values, beliefs, and rules presents challenges, but on the upside, this increases the child's adaptability to varied environments. Short-term reactions include considerable anxiety, as the child's world is destroyed and rebuilt in a fashion that they have no control over. Worrying about where parents are going, when the child will see them again, and greater existential questions such as "If my parents don't love each other anymore, does this mean they won't love me someday?" generates constant stress and anxiety. Small children may regress into seeking more attention from parents, bedwetting, or returning to negative behaviors. Adolescents can become angry, defiant, and rebel against parental authority.

Child risk factors for parental incarceration include child criminal involvement, physical problems and antisocial behavior, poor educational attainment, impaired economic well-being, and diminished parent-child attachment and contact while the parent is incarcerated. As the majority of incarcerated Americans are men, most research on the childhood effects of this life experience deal with the imprisonment of fathers, stepfathers, grandfathers, uncles, and male cousins. However, maternal incarceration has grown rapidly in recent years, and the number of children with a mother in prison increased 131 percent from 1991 to 2007, according to Glaze and Maruschak (2008). As the world's leader in incarceration, the United States saw a dramatic growth of 500 percent in the size of the prison population over the last forty years.

The U.S. criminal justice system is plagued by racial disparities and drug sentencing disparities. Almost 60 percent of the people in prison are people of color. Black and Hispanic men, who comprise a small percentage of the national population, are incarcerated at higher rates than white men. Incarceration poses difficulties for maintaining intimate and family relationships. Families find that making regular visits, phone calls, and sending letters and packages to their loved ones in prison can be difficult and costly. The financial burdens created by the incarcerated parent's inability to contribute to the family's budget exacerbate this situation. Families suffer economic insecurity and may deal with the hardship by using public assistance. Families feel emotional strain because they cannot connect with their incarcerated member's daily life and experiences. Maternal stress may affect a mother's ability to offer secure parent-child relationships.

Most mothers and fathers self-report that their children perform worse and experience learning difficulties after their father's incarceration. Foster and Hagan's research (2015) corroborates this anecdotal data. They discovered that parental incarceration decreases the educational attainment of children and contributes to their long-term social exclusion. Murray, Farrington, and Sekol (2012) suggest that the children of incarcerated parents experienced turmoil and upset prior to the parents' imprisonment, thus they are at risk for a variety of adverse behavioral outcomes. Also, they suggested that studies show parental incarceration is associated with a higher risk of children's antisocial behavior, but not for mental health problems, drug use, or poor educational performance. Gottlieb's research (2016) suggests that children who experience household incarceration in early adolescence are at greater risk of having a premarital first birth, particularly when the father or an extended family member is incarcerated. Nonmarital childbearing, particularly coupled with growing up in a single-parent household, suggests that children have low educational attainment, low economic security, and decreased physical and psychological well-being. Children with incarcerated parents experience a unique anxiety related to the cycles of jail time. Uncertainty about their parent's absence and return can potentially cause more stress than if the parent was serving a long-term prison sentence.

Wildeman (2013) researched the consequences of mass imprisonment on childhood inequality and found that the U.S. prison boom was a key driver of the growing racial disparities in child homelessness, thus increasing black-white inequality in this risk by 65 percent since the 1970s. Finally, gender plays a role in how a child feels the effects of parental incarceration. Girls and boys are socialized to process experiences in different ways. Girls internalize, while boys externalize. Externalizing includes aggression and acting out. Internalizing means that the child's feelings are displayed via sadness, sympathy, and anxiety. Brewer-Smith, Pohlig, and Bucurescu (2016) collated data from adult female prison inmates who had incarcerated parents during childhood. Their regression analyses of data revealed that for women, having incarcerated adult family members was related to greater frequency and severity of childhood abuse and a higher incidence of neurological deficits in adulthood, especially related to traumatic brain injuries, compared to those without incarcerated adult family members.

NEGLECT

Child neglect, both emotional and physical, comprises the majority of maltreatment reported to child protective services. The majority of American children enter the foster care system due to neglect. Homelessness and household insecurity are components of neglect. Having an incarcerated parent increases the likelihood of children entering foster care. In its most severe forms, emotional neglect can cause major physical and cognitive developmental delays. Its effect on the brain is irreversible. The prefrontal cortex fails to mature, which reduces the child's capacity for executive functioning—focus, sustained attention, decision-making, and problem-solving.

Neglectful parenting is also associated with mental illness and addiction. Poverty and social isolation are also associated with neglect. Emotional neglect occurs when parents fail to respond to a child's emotional needs. Parents' failure to validate their child's feelings results in the child feeling deeply alone and isolated. The children believe that the emotional neglect is their fault, they caused it, because they are too needy, too sensitive, or selfish. Neglect also involves parents not meeting their children's emotional needs. If a child asks for help, they are rebuffed and chided for being too sensitive or needy. Once conditioned to being shut down, emotionally neglected children never ask for help from a parent, caregiver, or anyone else because they have been taught that their needs are inconsequential. The types of parents who tend to emotionally neglect their children are authoritarian, narcissistic, perfectionist, or absent. They shame and humiliate their children. The emotional neglect of children results in lack of confidence, difficulty dealing with criticism, panic, and profound loneliness. Since the children are trained to have no needs or voice any emotional needs, they shut down, become emotionally numb, and experience difficulties feeling, identifying, managing, and communicating their emotions because the parents disavowed their expression of emotions they felt discomfited by.

Sometimes emotionally neglected children turn toward perfectionism as a means of being self-sufficient, unburdensome, and difficult to criticize for their failings. They can become oversensitive to rejection by taking everything personally. They also lack clarity about boundaries and expectations. All of these experiences can increase the risk of anxiety and depression, and deficits in emotion perception and emotional regulation. The children may be desensitized, have less empathy, and respond poorly to the emotional expressions of friends and family members. Emotional neglect by a parent arrests brain development. It makes attaching to others and having lasting, healthy adult relationships difficult because trusting others is challenging. Emotionally neglected children can have difficulties recognizing the facial expressions of others that show different emotions, thus diminishing their capacity for empathy, understanding, and connections with others. All of these outcomes of neglect can affect academic performance and intelligence.

Physical neglect refers to whether the child's basic and age-appropriate needs for food, clothing, shelter, and medical care are met by the parents. Physically neglected children may not be enrolled in school, or the parents may not monitor the child's attendance. Children are left alone at home for lengthy periods of time that exceed what is recommended by the American Academy of Pediatrics. Identifying physically neglected children can be easy. They are inappropriately dressed for the weather, appear dirty, smell unwashed, appear malnourished, and may display skin rashes, skin disorders, or bites from bedbugs and other vermin. Their behavior includes meager social skills, food stealing and hoarding, disinterest in basic hygiene, and poor school performance and attendance—including falling asleep in class. The children may show a severe lack of attachment to parents or other adults, and yet they can also be clingy and demand excessive attention and affection. Like other forms of abuse and neglect, physical neglect affects the physical, psychological, cognitive, and behavioral development of children. Developmental delays are customary and expected. Lack of boundaries is common because abused children find the limits set by adults and caregivers to be unfamiliar. The physical consequences of neglect can range from minor cuts and bruises to brain damage and death. The psychological outcomes can range from chronic low self-esteem to severe dissociative states. The cognitive effects also range from attention disorders to neurocognitive disorders. Behaviorally, physically neglected children may experience alienation from their peers or may exhibit disturbingly violent actions. All of these difficulties affect individual children and society as a whole.

Trauma and abuse stunt neurological development, leaving many children, and adult learners, emotionally functioning at levels well below their chronological ages. Figure 1.3 summarizes the many forms that adverse childhood experiences can take. Grownups can help children process adverse experiences that trigger feelings of loss and unworthiness. Those who provide unconditional love lay a groundwork for children to gain the skills for greater resilience.

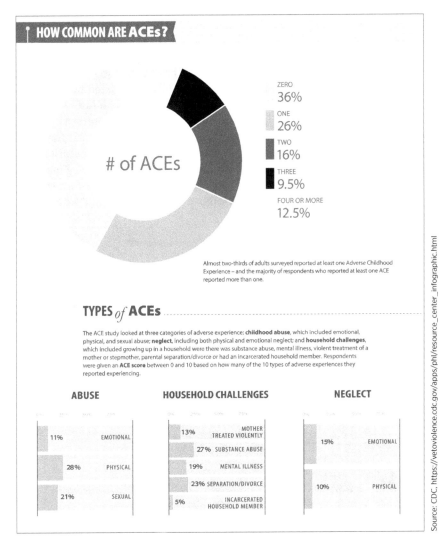

Source: CDC, https://vetoviolence.cdc.gov/apps/phl/resource_center_infographic.html

FIGURE 1.3

Types of ACEs

THE ACEs SCORE

The more ACEs that a person has suffered as a child, the higher their ACEs score. A high ACEs score correlates with intravenous drug use, alcoholism, chronic depression, rape, risky sexual behaviors, smoking, liver disease, homelessness, incarceration, diabetes, obesity, and other outcomes such as shorter life expectancy. In fact, people with six or more ACEs tend to die approximately twenty years earlier than their peers. Reviewing the ACEs pyramid (figure 1.4) informs us of the trajectory from ACEs to early death.

Adopting a trauma-informed framework transforms our perspective on people who are coping with these issues. Rather than dismissing their problems as inherited—though it is likely that inherited factors do play some role in a person's ACEs score, personality, mental health, and so on—we should understand that these outcomes are survival skills engendered by childhood trauma. Likewise, it is not always clear to the adult with a high ACEs score why these psychic wounds are triggered or re-traumatized years after the abuse occurred. The survivor may lack a perspective on normal familial functioning, or simply may not have received therapy. Likewise, their maturity level may be less than expected given their biological age. Finally, they may lack the capacity for self-reflection. When viewed through a trauma-informed lens, so-called peculiar behavior in our patrons can be recognized, and we can then

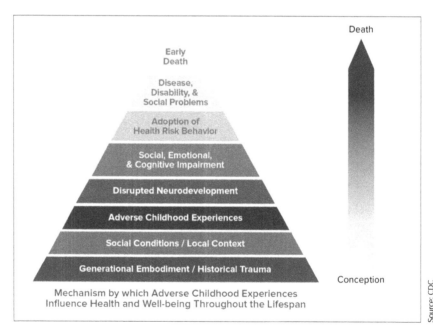

Mechanism by which Adverse Childhood Experiences Influence Health and Well-being Throughout the Lifespan

Source: CDC

FIGURE 1.4
The ACEs Pyramid

provide an emotionally safe environment in which their information needs are met with sensitivity and mindfulness. While librarians are not generally concerned with their patrons' morbidity and mortality, a knowledge of how ACEs scores affect the population we serve can help us to develop a holistic vision of a person. Developing empathy for adults with high ACEs is key to providing sensitive customer service from our desks, phones, mobile devices, and social media accounts. We can perceive that anger, belligerence, obscene language, banned behavior, or any other type of disruptive conduct in our library is most likely due to poor coping skills and brain chemistry. Library workers' knowledge of ACEs scores and their effects on the adult brain is the first step toward providing empathetic, trauma-informed customer services. This understanding adds another layer of insight to serving our clients with the care and compassion they both need and deserve.

Additionally, high ACEs scores affect society by taking an economic toll. For instance, the Centers for Disease Control estimates the lifetime cost of child maltreatment at $124 billion. This includes $83.5 billion lost in productivity costs, $25 billion in health care costs, $4.6 billion in special education, $4.4 billion in child welfare, and $3.9 billion in criminal justice. As adults, we may be re-traumatized by an event and need to absent ourselves from work. Workers without sick or annual leave must appear at work, but are distracted and anxious due to a re-traumatization, thus accounting for the lost productivity costs mentioned earlier. Increasing special education costs are understandable once we recognize the effects that traumatic childhood experiences can have upon a child's neurological development, comprehension, and learning. When adults with high ACEs scores have children, they must seek counseling for their trauma so they can prevent an intergenerational cycle of high ACEs. When these adults cannot develop self-regulation skills, their quality of life may decline, and their children may spend time in the child welfare system until the parents successfully work out a plan with their social worker. A study by Sun et al. (2017) determined that mothers' ACEs are significantly associated with their children's developmental risk, and some findings suggest that focusing on intergenerational trauma via the ACEs score of young children's caregivers may promote child improvement.

An ACEs scoring instrument is provided in appendix A for those interested in determining their personal ACEs score.

2

The Trauma-Informed Approach to Service

Trauma-informed care is a framework for understanding and responding to psychological trauma. Within the U.S. Department of Health and Human Services, the Substance Abuse and Mental Health Services Administration (SAMHSA) functions with the mission of reducing the effects of substance abuse and mental illness on our communities. Its Trauma and Justice Strategic Initiative of 2014 prepared guidelines outlining the concept of trauma and providing guidance for a trauma-informed approach within the context of human behavioral service delivery. SAMHSA developed the "three Es" and the "four Rs," mnemonics that help everyone recall key concepts in this care approach. The three Es refer to *events, experiences,* and *effects,* while the fours Rs relate to our key assumptions within a trauma-informed approach: *realization, recognize, respond,* and *resist re-traumatization.*

THE THREE Es

Traumatic events may happen once or they may occur chronically, thus contributing to an environment of toxic stress for a child or other individual. Exposure to one or more traumatic events is a diagnostic criterion. A person's emotional and cognitive experience of the event can govern whether it is, in fact, a traumatic event. A key predictor of whether a person's experience is traumatic involves the presence of a power differential. SAMHSA describes this as whether an individual, an event, or a force of nature has power over another. Feelings of betrayal, self-blame, humiliation, shame, and guilt play a large role in traumatic experiences. Furthermore, these traumatic experiences are related to cultural beliefs, social supports, and the developmental age of the person. The abuse of women and the experience of domestic violence are examples of how cultural beliefs around gender and biological sex can predict a traumatic experience. Having adequate social support in the form of loving family members, school counselors, or a faith community mitigates the experience of trauma. Finally, age plays a role in our understanding and self-reflection on events and also influences the adverse effects of trauma.

The effects of trauma may be immediate or delayed. They also vary along a spectrum of the short and the long term. Without therapy and self-reflection, those suffering from the adverse effects of trauma may not realize the cause of their distress and other symptoms. SAMHSA describes both visible and invisible effects, such as a person's inability to cope with the normal stresses and pressures of daily life; to trust and benefit from relationships; to manage cognitive processes, such as memory, attention, and thinking; to regulate behavior; and to control the expression of emotions.

THE FOUR Rs

Key assumptions in a trauma-informed approach include the four Rs mentioned above. The first step is to realize the ubiquity of trauma. A trauma-informed library recognizes the signs and symptoms of trauma in its staff and in the people they serve. Library administrators, librarians, and staff can respond empathically to the experience of trauma by fully integrating our understanding of trauma into the library's policies, procedures, practices, and services. By doing these things, the trauma-informed library resists re-traumatization and adjusts its customer service models accordingly. We realize that customer service is complicated and should meet users where they are, without our assumptions and expectations predicting or guiding a typical exchange or transaction. Instead of asking "What is wrong with them?" we should reframe and ask "What happened to them?" and then serve their needs with empathy.

First and foremost, trauma-informed care emphasizes safety for providers and survivors, but it also assumes that the people we serve, as well as our own workforce, more than likely have a history of trauma. Trauma-informed care embraces an understanding of trauma and an awareness of the effect it can have across settings, services, and populations. This includes recognizing the signs and symptoms of trauma in students, other members of the communities we serve, and ourselves. Another aspect of trauma-informed care of particular interest to libraries is that it requires vigilance in anticipating and avoiding institutional processes and practices that may re-traumatize individuals with histories of trauma. Such an approach requires administrators to integrate a basic understanding of trauma into the library's policies, procedures, and practices. Finally, one of the most essential aspects, and one particularly appealing to librarians promoting a user-experience perspective, is the patrons' collaboration and participation in the development, delivery, and evaluation of customer services.

ORIGINS OF TRAUMA-INFORMED CARE

While symptoms of traumatic stress have always been with us, the earliest modern accounts of the symptoms extend as far back as the American Civil War. And the roots of trauma-informed care lie within that of PTSD, which has a clear mind-body connection. The term *soldier's heart* was used in the nineteenth and twentieth centuries to describe veterans' susceptibility to cardiovascular disease, which, in effect, linked physical disease with what we now call PTSD. After the Civil War, numerous physicians tackled the idea of nervousness and its effects on physical health. *Beard's Practical Treatise on Nervous Exhaustion (Neurasthenia)* (1884) was an early book conceptualizing the idea that one's brain has a great effect upon physical health.

Much of early twentieth-century thought on the topic was informed by efforts to treat war veterans suffering from *shell shock*, a condition which we now know as PTSD. Sigmund Freud's notions about the emotional roots of hysterical symptoms were often applied to soldiers suffering from shell shock and other "war neuroses." Soldiers presenting somatic symptoms like paralysis, joint stiffness, and loss of speech and senses were regarded as suffering from conversion hysteria. With World War II the growth of psychosomatic medicine accelerated, and veterans were routinely served by expanded and enhanced psychiatric care that the previous generation of soldiers had to seek out on their own personal initiative.

Back on the home front, early twentieth-century workers dealt with the aftermath of industrial and railway accidents. These first-generation approaches to serving veterans and workers eventually extended to those healing from natural disasters, terrorism, and refugees fleeing human rights violations. However, PTSD was not included in the *Diagnostic and Statistical Manual of Mental Disorders* (*DSM*) until after 1980. The influx of Vietnam veterans presenting with severe symptoms convinced *DSM-III* to include the disorder, but feminist activists and therapists, who had been working with survivors on intimate partner and sexual violence, were quick to point out that PTSD was not only suffered by veterans but had been observed for decades in survivors of domestic abuse.

Some of the problems with the *DSM-III* was how it defined trauma as an event outside the range of normal human experience, and many feminists and feminist social workers critiqued this as inaccurate. One of the purposes, or desired outcomes, of educating people about the promise of trauma-informed approaches is that trauma is normalized. The term *normalization* refers to a process that makes something seem less atypical or unusual. Public discussions of childhood trauma help bring the issue into the open and may encourage conversations at many levels. However, the stigma and shame around abuse and trauma make it difficult for many people to discuss these experiences publicly or privately or admit to themselves that they are survivors. Those informed about trauma-informed care treat everyone as though they've experienced trauma, so that the stigma surrounding our universal experiences lessens.

Another criticism of the *DSM* is how it represents a middle-class, white, and male perspective on normalcy. We should keep in mind that the definition of PTSD didn't capture the complexities of our vulnerability to trauma, and the effects on our identity both during and after traumatization. Nor did it consider the effects of the social environment on increasing the risk of trauma. Further, Burstow (2003) says that we can't understand PTSD symptoms unless we also examine individual lives and how social structures and institutions affect populations. This aspect of thinking about trauma and PTSD aligns with ACRL's Diversity Standards: Cultural Competency for Academic Libraries, discussed in chapter 3.

PTSD affects people who experience war, natural disasters, terrorism, bullying, and school shootings, but it also affects people, especially children, who live in homes characterized by neglect, intimate partner violence, addiction, physical, emotional, or sexual abuse, and the traumatic loss of a parent or loved one to death, divorce, or incarceration. PTSD can be triggered by anything a person senses: vision, scent, hearing, and so on. This involuntary reexperiencing of the original trauma sends the person through a cycle of anxiety, panic, and flashbacks. They can be hyper-aroused and hypervigilant to their environment in order to anticipate and defend themselves from experiencing additional trauma. The *DSM-V* criteria for PTSD include reexperiencing, avoidance, negative cognitions and mood, and arousal. All of these symptoms are easy to identify in our users once we understand how the symptoms manifest in individuals.

THREE PILLARS OF TRAUMA-INFORMED CARE

According to Bath (2008), the three pillars of trauma-informed care are safety, connection, and emotional management. Since 1998 the effects of trauma on children have increasingly become the concern of social services, education, health care, and law enforcement. Bath and Greenwald (2005) posit that healing from trauma often happens in nonclinical settings, and that in fact often the majority of healing comes from children's direct interactions with parents, counselors, teachers, coaches, direct care workers, and case managers. This type of healing has great implications for librarianship as well. Librarians teach, coach, counsel, and refer users to other professionals. Our roles and locations within our organization position us as a workforce that can foster healing from trauma by means of our spaces and our operations. Fred Rogers, better known as Mister Rogers, the preschool television personality, is often quoted as saying, "If you could only sense how important you are to the lives of those you meet; how important you can be to the people you may never dream of. There is something of yourself that you leave at every meeting with another person."

Creating safe spaces for trauma survivors is essential. While we librarians generally are not responsible for the emotional safety of our users, we can control elements of physical safety by making changes to physical spaces, like interiors and exteriors, as well as closely examining our policies, procedures, and processes for their potential to re-traumatize users. Trauma-informed care emphasizes personal control over users' circumstances in the library where this is reasonable and practical, and we can alter our built environment in ways that allow us to ensure their safety.

Once secure spaces are established and maintained, additional safety is created by connections and relationship development between library patrons and library staff. Having libraries of all kinds trained in trauma-informed care can help us both intervene in the under-eighteen populations we serve, and also not re-traumatize adults. The qualities of positive relationships between adults and children directly inform the latter's resilience. Mutual respect, trust, honesty, and good communication are a few of these qualities. Coincidentally, these qualities overlap with the principles of trauma-informed care.

A TRAUMA-INFORMED TRANSFORMATION

Trauma-informed approaches can be used to design and transform our service systems. They allow library users authoritative roles in the design, deployment, and assessment of customer service. When library users present their information need, we serve them without any knowledge of their individual trauma histories. Our lack of awareness and empathy can result in miscommunication on our part, feeling misunderstood on their part, and all individuals left stymied and possibly re-traumatized. Trauma survivors may leave our libraries feeling vulnerable. We should prevent these negative turnaways. While many of us may be familiar with expressions of sympathy for our library clients, we should actually change our approach to easing any pain and suffering we encounter while serving our communities.

Brené Brown (2013) makes a clear distinction between sympathy and empathy that is helpful, relevant, and easily applicable within trauma-informed approaches to customer service. Brown says: "Empathy fuels connection. Sympathy drives disconnection." Brown cites Wiseman's (1996) work on empathy, which noted the four attributes of empathy: perspective-taking, refraining from judgment, recognizing emotions, and communication. Brown encapsulates these four attributes in the statement "Empathy is feeling with people." Brown explains that when someone is in a negative space/place, we can express empathy by acknowledging that we've been in the same place and we know what it's like. On the other hand, sympathy is us telling the person suffering how bad it is and offering them a sandwich. It's feeling sorry for another person. Or when talking to someone who has miscarried a pregnancy, telling them "At least you can get pregnant again." Or any response beginning with "At least. . .": "At least your cancer is treatable," "At least you still have a home." Brown calls this strategy "silverlining": when we try to help someone out of their funk by pushing them to the bright side when they're clearly unready. Another example of sympathy, not empathy, is one-upping the patron with your own sob story: "Your house burned down? Mine burned down three times." Or someone saying, "That happened to my mother and she handled it this way. . . ." Choosing and responding with empathy requires both emotional intelligence and emotional vulnerability. Brown said that responses don't make things better, connecting with another person does.

Librarians cannot address the symptoms or syndromes related to the type of abuse our users have experienced, but we can and should provide customer service that is welcoming, grounded in safety, appropriate, and which considers the special needs of trauma survivors. Harris and Fallot (2001) provide an analogy explaining blurred boundaries between systems, which oversee guidelines and services that provide access to physical spaces. This analogy may be useful for understanding the model:

> The Americans with Disabilities Act (1990) mandated that a wide range of civic and cultural organizations construct their environments so that events are accessible to persons with a range of special needs. As a result, concerts and museums now provide wheelchair access, most theaters have at least one performance that is signed for the hearing impaired, and convenient parking for restaurants is set aside for patrons who cannot walk long distances. These organizations are not delivering specific services for persons with disabilities. Instead, by becoming "disability informed," they are making their services truly available to all people.

Mental health organizations and therapists are expected to care for trauma-tized individuals. However, outside of that milieu, trends in care demonstrate that systems of child welfare, education, health care, juvenile justice, and first responders like emergency medical technicians and law enforcement offi-cers are incorporating trauma-informed perspectives into their service phi-losophy and practices. Key elements of implementation include relying on evidence-based practices, educating care providers and making information available to them, and ensuring a continuity of care across these systems.

Each system takes a different approach to serving traumatized individuals. Once a child is traumatized, they increasingly rely on services from the afore-mentioned organizations. In fact, traumatic stress is also associated with an increased use of health and mental health services and increased involvement with other child-serving systems, such as the child welfare and juvenile justice systems. Child-serving systems need a knowledgeable workforce, steadfast organizations, and expert professionals. Many libraries and their workers are child-serving, specifically school libraries and public libraries. Moreover, some academic and special libraries may have child-centered collections or areas or may welcome patrons of all ages to their outreach and programming.

SERVICE WITHOUT LABELS

Public and school librarians have always been responsive to trauma-induced behaviors, even when they were not recognized as such. The main exam-ple in public libraries is their outreach and service to those experiencing homelessness. In the past, librarians dealt with the homeless by expelling them from libraries, but over time the protocol around homeless people has changed in public libraries, and now we incorporate their needs into our pro-grams, services, and outreach. Public libraries are pulled between serving the information (and other) needs of the homeless, and those of the adequately housed who feel uncomfortable with the visible signs of homelessness they or their children encounter at public libraries. In the past, librarians sided with the housed, since they pay the taxes that support funding for libraries. But favoring one group of users over another is antithetical to our Code of Ethics, which calls for the equitable treatment of everyone using our collec-tions and services. This binary sets up a clear inequality of expectations that doesn't necessarily have a basis in reality or allow for personal variety: for example, the pleasant homeless patron and the unpleasant but adequately housed patron. Our users who are homeless typically fall into the category of "problem patrons," which is discussed later with regard to using inclusive language and reframing how our profession characterizes normality and normal behavior.

Ferrell (2010) used work on labeling in nursing literature as a new frame-work for examining the idea of the "problem patron" in professional library practice. She urged librarians to reexamine how we approach challenging patron situations. She essentially suggests that we librarians adopt a high level of cultural competence in determining our values and norms, and adjust our expectations, policies, and procedures accordingly, which aligns perfectly with trauma-informed practices and approaches. If we assume that a majority of librarians understand the norms and expectations of society, and that they can and do operate within those boundaries, then it is reasonable to assume that a majority would also support the norm, the adequately housed, as opposed to those experiencing homelessness. In other words, because they are adequately housed themselves, they may advocate more strongly for the rights of taxpayers who are property owners, rather than people experiencing homelessness.

It seems that public libraries handle the "overflow" resulting from homelessness, as Simmons (1985) has suggested. Simmons said that if our social services infrastructure met all the needs of the homeless, then public libraries would not be heavily used by them as places for respite and sanctuary. Provence (2019) discussed how public libraries currently partner with health departments and social service agencies for needs assessment, outreach, and referral services. Some universities and public libraries now place social work students in libraries as interns and for practicums.

Regardless of how we feel or react to "problem patrons," ALA clearly outlines librarians' responsibilities to the homeless in Policy 61, Library Services to the Poor:

> It is crucial that libraries recognize their role in enabling poor people to participate fully in a democratic society, by utilizing a wide variety of available resources and strategies. Concrete programs of training and development are needed to sensitize and prepare library staff to identify poor people's needs and deliver relevant services. (American Library Association 2010)

BETTER OUTCOMES WITH TRAUMA-INFORMED CARE

Over the past decades, human services organizations have evolved their systems to incorporate trauma theory and trauma-informed care approaches. Organizations providing health care, mental health care, and substance abuse treatment lost clients because their systems failed; rising numbers of dropouts from treatment programs, declines in successful outcomes, and high costs caused policymakers to reexamine their delivery systems. Vivian Brown (2018) examined the problem and discovered that the organizations which transformed their services into trauma-informed ones experienced more successful outcomes with clients. Brown believes that effective organizational change must include trauma-informed practice and that trauma-informed practice will eventually evolve into standard practice.

Furthermore, Brown delineates specific populations that are at high risk of experiencing traumatic events and at high risk of re-traumatization. Brown lists these populations as women (pregnant women, postpartum women, women who have lost custody of a child/children, and women who have experienced domestic violence); men who are survivors of sexual and physical abuse; individuals living with HIV/AIDS; children (those in the child welfare system, those who have incarcerated parents, and those experiencing childhood adversity); and lesbian, gay, bisexual, and transgender individuals. While some members of these populations may be easy to identify visually, it's best that librarians and library staff providing customer service simply treat every patron with the same level of empathy and care.

STAFF BEHAVIOR

Richardson (n.d.) offers trauma-informed guidelines for staff behavior. Most of these guidelines include aspects of professional behavior that we naturally learn as professionals and adhere to such as respect and proper manners, responsiveness to requests for help, minimizing delays, active listening, clear and typical speech patterns, friendly eye contact, a pleasant demeanor, welcoming nonverbal communication, and initiation of greetings. Privacy and confidentiality of library patron information are also central to our professional values, and while we're aware of this, all who use our spaces, services, and collections may not understand our professional ethics. Introducing library patrons to our vow of protecting their privacy should be a part of any conversation that we have with them. Pointedly averting our eyes when patrons log into desktops, laptops, or cloud-based accounts is essential. Some library staff may opt to express this verbally as well by saying, "I'll look away while you log in."

Another area in which library workers should take care is that of respecting patrons' personal boundaries. You should ask the patron's consent to demonstrate a search strategy on their personal laptop or on the library's equipment, and consent is also needed to touch or guide the person—especially if they are someone with a visual disability or are only partially sighted—to another area of the library. Likewise, offering water or some other beverage is okay, but library staff should not eat or drink while helping, since this may trigger a trauma survivor.

We, as librarians serving populations of children, teens, and adults from a variety of economic backgrounds, religions, and ethnic origins, need to acknowledge an additional, invisible layer of identity—our patrons' ACEs score. Surviving a history of physical, sexual, or emotional abuse, as well as serious illnesses and negative experiences in institutionalized settings, can affect trauma survivors' interactions with professionals in all areas of their lives. We should respond with empathy and sensitivity to all of the communities we serve because those values of service tie in to the Library Bill of Rights' last two policies: "V. A person's right to use a library should not be denied or abridged because of origin, age, background, or views," and "VI. Libraries which make exhibit spaces and meeting rooms available to the public they serve should make such facilities available on an equitable basis, regardless of the beliefs or affiliations of individuals or groups requesting their use" (American Library Association 1996). The ALA's various interpretations of the Library Bill of Rights include a range of philosophies, but the interpretation on "Equity, Diversity, Inclusion" addresses the library workforce, saying that we should embrace equity, diversity, and inclusion in all of our service philosophies and operations.

Furthermore, transitioning to a trauma-informed organizational culture helps library workforces smooth over the rough edges when their staff members exhibit abrasive behavior. Finally, the emphasis on administrative support of the workforce's self-care is something that all who work in academic libraries can benefit from as a means of preventing burnout, secondary traumatization, and impaired functioning.

3

Trauma-Informed Care and Libraries

Trauma-informed care and libraries infusing trauma-informed principles in our libraries' customer service approaches is appropriate and timely given the beliefs underlying our profession's Code of Ethics, as well as recent staffing and collaboration trends in public and academic libraries. How can we uphold our Code of Ethics, which states that we provide the highest level of equitable, unbiased, and courteous service to all users, when the language we use to describe "problem patrons" sets up an oppositional dynamic from the start? How can we truly serve all information needs when our familiarity with resources is limited to our print and electronic resources, which may not offer local help and referral to our community members in need of information, like where to find a local food pantry, how to secure a safe place to sleep for the night, or other social services that many library staff have zero professional knowledge or personal experience with?

In the early 2000s, the city and county of San Francisco incorporated a library social work position into their operations to help people experiencing homelessness at the San Francisco Public Library. Students majoring in social work at San Jose State University worked in a pilot program at the San Jose Public Library in October 2009. Since then, administrators, librarians, and library staff have welcomed social workers to their organizations where they provide a host of services and referrals to users but depart from the tried-and-true case management associated with their workflow. Large urban public library systems have begun to hire social workers who then refer targeted library users to meaningful and appropriate social services. Elissa Hardy, a community resource specialist at the Denver Public Library, is notable for her support and training of library staff, her management of three social workers on staff at the system, and her adjunct teaching at the University of Denver's Graduate School of Social Work to distinguish a new social work domain.

Surprisingly, the majority of collaborations between social workers and libraries are initiated by the former, and more specifically, by social work faculty at universities. Tracy M. Soska, an associate professor at the University of Pittsburgh's School of Social Work, compares the expanded roles of public libraries with the Progressive Era's settlement house legacy. Smaller and nonpublic organizations lack the funds to fill professional library staff positions, so hiring a social worker is impossible for most libraries. Instead, information professionals working in libraries can receive professional development education and training in the TIC approaches that social workers practice in their job, use these skills with library users, and thereby cover the customer service gap.

Zettervall and Nienow's excellent book *Whole Person Librarianship: A Social Work Approach to Patron Services* (2019) covers the intersection of librarianship and social work practice. It describes how social work's concepts like relationship-based services, sustainability, self-care, reflective practice, and cultural humility should be applied to librarianship. It does not advocate using a trauma-informed or trauma-responsive lens, as I do, but the authors' approach aligns the sister professions of librarianship and social work with each other by focusing primarily on social work. Alternatively, trauma-informed systems are interdisciplinary in form and multidisciplinary in practice.

CODE OF ETHICS

Librarians uphold the values and beliefs established by our professional organizations. Those beliefs and values underlie our passion for and interest in serving the information needs of our populations. Specifically, ALA's Library Code of Ethics created in 1939, and most recently updated in 2008, outlines eight guiding principles. Several are germane to the context of library customer service being trauma-informed, which in turn imbues empathy in our professional practice. The first principle, mentioned earlier, emphasizes equity, lack of bias on behalf of the library staff, and courteousness. Providing the highest level of service without an understanding of trauma-informed principles is impossible. Equitable access cannot be provided when we inadvertently trigger a traumatic response in our users. Likewise, our relationships with our colleagues affect the type of customer service we provide. Dysfunctional organizational cultures and toxic organizational behaviors directly affect the tenor of services provided by library workers. Our Code of Ethics' fifth principle states: *We treat co-workers and other colleagues with respect, fairness, good faith, and advocate for conditions of employment that safeguard the rights and welfare of all employees of our institutions.*

Principles seven and eight provide additional support for libraries' adoption of trauma-informed approaches to customer service. Many of us are taught by our parents, institutions, popular culture, and the media to believe that problems like homelessness, addiction, mental health issues, poverty, and self-harm are personal failings due to weak character or weak morals. We're taught that these conditions happen to those who bring it on themselves through their bad choices, poor impulse control, or ill-informed and irrational decision-making. A trauma-informed approach to customer service recognizes that behaviors and issues like the aforementioned ones are symptoms of ACEs, rather than of moral failings.

Despite what our personal beliefs may be about our users' failings, adopting a trauma-informed approach is consistent with adherence to the Code of Ethics' seventh principle, in which we *distinguish between our personal convictions and professional duties and do not allow our personal beliefs to interfere with fair representation of the aims of our institution or the provision of access to its information resources.* Our profession's language for the behaviors and issues we experience with certain populations—"problem patrons," "difficult patrons," or "atypical patrons"—creates barriers to serving our users equitably. This negative terminology frames these issues so that our assumptions, intentions, and expectations from encounters with "problem patrons" set us up for failure in serving their information needs. Until our customer service philosophy, library and information science education, and professional literature address our professional bias against "problem patrons" and adopt inclusive language, we will leave our users unserved.

Additionally, those familiar with the Association of College and Research Libraries' (ACRL's) Diversity Standards: Cultural Competency for Academic Libraries can see how those standards (adopted in 2012) support a trauma-informed approach to customer service. Under the first standard, "cultural awareness of self and others," information professionals working in libraries should "develop an understanding of their own personal and cultural values and beliefs as a first step in appreciating the importance of multicultural identities in the lives of the people they work with and serve" (Association of College and Research Libraries 2012) This standard advises us to "guard against stereotyping" and become self-aware by means of self-reflection. Most TIC workshops and training offer an opportunity for participants to assess their individual trauma experienced prior to their eighteenth birthday. Post-assessment participants' awareness of how early childhood traumas can affect their lives can be eye-opening, humbling, and empathy-building. Having these "aha" moments can transform our personal lives, our professional lives, and ultimately results in empathy-driven customer services in libraries of all types. The third diversity standard addresses "organizational and professional values" and their importance to "user-focused service." It includes each area of library infrastructure, from public service to policymaking, administration, and managerial practice, which mirrors trauma-informed principles that situate the most important change within policies, procedures, and practices.

Returning to our professional Code of Ethics, its eighth principle suggests that our professional efficacy evolves and develops by *maintaining and enhancing our own knowledge and skills, by encouraging the professional development of co-workers, and by fostering the aspirations of potential members of the profession.* Growing our professional awareness of the approaches, like trauma-informed ones, that are employed by other helping professions can positively affect the quality of customer service in our libraries. This knowledge and training provide an opportunity for ongoing professional development and are also essential in the onboarding process for any new library staff we bring into our organization.

CUSTOMER SERVICE IN LIBRARIES

There are so many approaches to customer service in libraries. For the most part, these approaches focus on altering the behavior of individuals who serve the public—staff, librarians, volunteers, student workers, and graduate assistants. The approaches structured around our staff adhere to the Reference and User Services Association's (RUSA's) guidelines for serving and engaging our communities. A trauma-informed approach differs from RUSA's emphasis on training workers how to appropriately conduct themselves because of the significance it places on change in the organization at all levels, whereas RUSA's goals involve setting individual professional standards for behavior.

A trauma-informed approach begins with education. Here's a problem: a majority of our patrons have experienced trauma. Instead of labeling them as "disruptive" or "abnormal," let's regard them with empathy and understand that they're doing the best they can and that their adaptive behaviors seem completely reasonable and normal to them. One disconnect fueling our customer service failures is our perspective that these patrons' behaviors are problematic, disruptive, or even mentally disturbed. And then there is our assumption that "normal" people don't act out against community standards normalizing politeness, etiquette, and comportment. But once everyone in the organization realizes that our ingrained beliefs about behavior being "good," "bad," or "unacceptable" or falling anywhere along that continuum is a destructive point of view, then the organization itself can change. An organization should change its policies and procedures and practices so that they are empathy-driven and trauma-informed. If approached methodically, over time, this approach shows much promise in transforming an organization's functioning so that staffers can better interact with our patrons in authentic, trauma-responsive ways.

Trends in new service models, which remove the reference desk, or streamline all services to one point, rather than having one desk in each department, section, or floor of the building, are occurring across our libraries. Most of the trends and new ideas concerning customer service focus on changes to space and doing more with less: less space, less personnel, less operations. If we change our space and combine service desks, then patrons may feel as though all their needs are being met at one service point without going through needless and time-consuming referrals or the stock phrase "I can't help you with that." When libraries ask their staff to change their behavior, they're asking for a display of politeness, courtesy, engagement, or interest that our patrons experience as sincere—or that we hope are perceived as sincere. But being told simply to "be nicer" or "connect with each patron with warmth on a personal level" is a surface fix. It implies that all our customer service issues can be fixed by blanket instructions for everyone to act with the same robotic sweetness to all patrons. These two ideas, or trends, may cause strife. Library workers who may have previously only checked out items to patrons now expect to have expanded conversations while determining information needs vis-à-vis the reference interview. Being held to new behavioral expectations in the library workplace can be stressful. Asking all library workers to smile and project cheer and helpfulness can tax a person's emotional labor limits. Another issue in this specific scenario is that disparate service models are competing. Typically, circulation is about explaining policy and placing limits on patrons' ability to access material, such as, if they don't have a library card in hand, they cannot check out materials. However, service philosophy of reference differs in that policy and limitations rarely enter the conversation, as reference librarians meet the information needs of the person, sometimes breaking the rules. At my academic library, while reference books aren't allowed to be checked out, the head of reference regularly made exceptions for faculty who needed to check out and remove a reference work from the library for personal use or use in their classroom.

The traditional emphasis has been on tweaking employees' behavior without addressing their underlying philosophies or generating authentic empathy for patrons. Yohn (2019) said people are five times more likely to recommend a company or make future purchases if their experience as a customer was good. But what is a good customer service experience? Jordan (2005) described it as a special feeling that serving patrons is more than just another task to complete in the course of the library staff's day. Jordan expands on this and asks patrons whether they feel that the organization is designed around their needs. Another way of describing this is asking hard questions about all aspects of the library, not just the public service desks where people are being helped one on one.

BECOMING USER-CENTERED

Many libraries are process-oriented rather than user-oriented. Being process-oriented is a relic of the old way of structuring and organizing libraries which posits the librarian or library staffer as the person around whom use and access orbit. But libraries are changing and are moving toward user-centric models for access and operations. This is a problem when we claim to be user-oriented on the surface, but not deeply within our processes.

This issue came up recently in an all-faculty and staff meeting at my academic library. The minutes from the last meeting were clarified around confusion regarding book jackets. Some libraries use book covers (or dust jackets) for displays because the covers often display images and elements of design and typography which draw the eye and attract attention to the display or encourage people to use and borrow the books. Our library does not. Our practice during physical processing is to security—strip the spines, bar-code the book, and separate the book from the book cover. The book covers are retained and are sometimes randomly used in displays or in glass display cases adjacent to the stacks area where the books are shelved. But book covers are not kept on the books that circulate. There is no set procedure for their retention, thus they are unorganized, and a comprehensive knowledge of what book covers we have, and their location is virtually impossible. Most people realize that marketing and advertising serve a valuable purpose across industries. Effective book jackets promote books to our patrons in a way that plain book covers alone cannot. However, the cataloger argued against changing our library's process from current practice to one that effectively shows and markets new books to patrons, because doing so would interrupt the staff's workflow. Additionally, shelving books with book jackets was considered by the cataloger to be cost-prohibitive because each cover would require more physical processing and an adjustable, plastic book jacket.

But to put this in context, this is a non-issue. The number of new print books that we order and receive is negligible. Additionally, we go through the physical process of adding security strips to physical materials. Our security gates haven't functioned properly for the past five to ten years, and our circulation staff tell people who set off the alarms as they leave to simply keep on moving through. Those working the first floor AskUs (former circulation desk) are trained to wave everyone along when and if the security gate beeps. First, we know that the gate beeps for many things, not just for our security-stripped books: guns, knives, and other metal objects. In an effort to not stigmatize or traumatize people leaving the building, library staff wave them through the exit doors and do not search their bags, parcels, or persons. So, if we're not searching bags and backpacks for stolen library material, why are we wasting staff processing time on adding security strips, and why are we wasting money on purchasing security strips?

The dichotomies present in the practices and policies of our library's cataloging unit are deep and wide. At this level, resistance to change is common. Arguments about change and cost savings usually stymie practical adjustments that can move our libraries toward the user-centric model we support—unless, that is, these adjustments don't cost anything or make anyone change a deeply embedded historical practice, process, or workflow. People are so wedded to following outdated practices and policies that they defend wasteful workflows and cannot turn a critical eye upon operations.

EVALUATING CUSTOMER SERVICE

Jordan (2005) believes that most public libraries lack follow-through when examining their customer services and evaluating them. The main reason for this, she says, is that public libraries fail customers because they are blind to the customer's experience. She finds that this failure isn't due to the organization's policies, procedures, and practices, but to its evaluation and assessment of its customer services. Jordan developed a measure, the Friendliness Factor, and selected thirty public libraries to visit using her evaluation system. Essentially, she worked as an undercover "mystery shopper" to gauge each library's rating. She discovered many barriers to service, including difficulty using chat services, bounced e-mail addresses when she asked reference questions, or even worse, no response. Jordan's negative experiences with face-to-face customer service varied tremendously, and ranged from working with harried, understaffed librarians to encountering people who never welcomed, acknowledged, or spoke to her. Being blind to the patron's experience is addressed by trauma-informed care, which recommends seeing library services through a TIC lens post-training or by asking trauma survivors to walk through the process for entering the building, asking for help, and trying to get a library card; basically all of the processes a new patron may experience.

Interestingly, Stephanie Covington, a clinician and consultant in the development and implementation of gender-responsive and trauma-informed services in both the public and private sectors, suggested this very practice, "the mystery shopper," in a recent conference, "Addressing Adverse Childhood Experiences—A Call to Action." She said that people providing services to trauma survivors usually do not recognize the barriers they face in receiving the help they need. She suggests that administrators and practitioners call their organization to see how easy getting an appointment is. What barriers do they face? A phone tree that is impossible to navigate, or that is never answered by a real, live human being? Is there a message informing callers to hit 0 for operator? Or is there an assumption that everyone should know this already? Making this type of assumption creates a barrier to service. When someone calls and asks how to get to your library, can you tell them how to use public transportation to your location? Covington (2018) suggests walking through the library's external and internal areas with our eyes open for barriers. Sometimes it is impossible to see things that we've ignored or taken for granted for many years. Having fresh eyes examine the library is most helpful. Library workers with a beginner's mindset are valuable for this process, as are new employees. As part of onboarding, asking new hires what potential service barriers they spot is another way to uncover this valuable, hidden information. Many of these approaches are discussed later in chapter 5 on safety and chapter 9 on empowerment, voice, and choice. Covington also cautions people about closing doors when clients/patrons are in our offices. We may do so for safety, but closed doors may trigger someone and make them feel unsafe, as if there are no means for escape.

It's probable that the key to effective library customer service is a bit of both areas: organizational policies, procedures, and practices, and evaluation and assessment practices. A trauma-informed approach effectively combines both of these areas and offers promise for solving the customer service failures that Jordan discovered.

4

The Trauma-Informed Library Environment

The library's building and grounds send a message to the community. The public library leader Pam Sandlian Smith recognized this when she came to the West Palm Beach Public Library in the 1990s. She immediately went to work upgrading the facility. The environment is significant within trauma-informed approaches to customer service. The trauma-informed approach encourages not only taking a hard look at your library inside and out from the perspective of patrons, but also its odors and sounds.

TRANSFORMATION AT THE WEST PALM BEACH PUBLIC LIBRARY

The first paragraph in Smith's article "Mildly Delirious Libraries: Transforming Your Library from Top to Bottom" painted a very dismal portrait of public libraries. "You wander in out of curiosity and get an overwhelming sense of disrepair, old furnishings, and confused organization. The carpet is dirty, the beige paint is chipping" (Smith 2008, 19). She's describing the West Palm Beach Public Library in the late 1990s when she took over as library director.

Smith said that the building telegraphed "irrelevant." She cleaned house, literally and figuratively, by refreshing the décor, weeding the collection, and encouraging those staff members who clung to the negative, stagnant legacy organizational culture to find employment elsewhere.

Transforming the library's physical environment was essential, since its environs and ambiance still suggested a sense of bleakness. Smith tapped a local person who developed a process called GASP (Graphics, Ambiance, Style, and Presentation) to rehab the space to match the employees' enthusiasm. Everyone worked together to select carpeting that matched the shared vision for the library: tropical, crisp, and fluid. Smith determined that the process of changing interiors affected employees and patrons alike. During the rehab process they developed a shared language which influenced their design process and spilled over into general library operations as they revitalized the library's space with the aim of making their community joyful.

I share this story because the library's physical environment is significant within trauma-informed approaches to customer service. Space, ambiance, and attention to detail matter, as demonstrated by Smith's experience at the West Palm Beach Public Library. "Appearances count," she says:

> When a library looks worn out, it can be more easily dismissed as non-essential. If we want our public to take the library seriously, we have to respect ourselves enough to invest in regular physical maintenance and upgrades, fresh paints and colors, clean furnishings, and tidy surroundings. Looking good is not an option, it is a requirement. (Smith 2008, 30)

Public libraries may have more leeway for having the built environment match the organizational vision. Other kinds of libraries may be rigidly bound by institutional branding and may not be allowed any freedom in making their spaces feel engaging or invigorating.

ALL FIVE SENSES

Examining our buildings, services, and environs using sight, smell, touch, sound, and taste offers a way to create welcoming spaces for everyone. It also allows us to correct what we can in order to make everyone feel welcome and safe within our libraries.

Visual examination of the parking areas, signage, and spaces includes noticing barriers to entry and removing or reducing them as much as possible. The language used on signs or by library staff should be inclusive, free of value judgments and stigma, and positive, not punitive. Are the library's grounds well-maintained and manicured? Regular maintenance may require patrons' exposure to intrusive mowing and blowing noises, the odor of cut grass, the possibility of cut grass landing on them, and walking through a cloud of cut grass, leaves, weeds, and dust to simply enter the library building. How easily do the library's doors open and close? Are the entryways well-lit and free from detritus?

Consider the smells upon entering and leaving the building. How close are the cigarette urns? Must patrons walk through clouds of cigarette fumes upon leaving and entering the building? What flowers, bushes, trees, and herbs are blooming? Planting soothing herbs like lavender, comfrey, and rosemary adjacent to exterior buildings may induce a positive experience in patrons.

How well does your library space pass the odor test? What pleasant and unpleasant odors are easily identified? How odorless are the bathrooms? How often are the bathrooms serviced by cleaning staff? What inoffensive, sustainable, odor-masking solutions are available? Does the smell of rot, mildew, or mold permeate offices or storage spaces that the public may access?

Odors are tricky given how very personal individuals' reactions to them may be. What is the library's policy on employees' use of perfumes, lotions, essential oils, and shampoos? Within the confines of my office space, I use an essential oil diffuser filled with peppermint as a preventative for daily headaches. When it is in use, a peppermint aroma fills the shared office space. Most everyone finds it pleasant, but the smell could trigger a trauma survivor. Colleagues drink coffee and tea daily in their offices. A shared coffeemaker behind the circulation desk operates each morning, filling the area with the smell of coffee. Many doctors' offices and hospitals are fragrance-free zones due to patients' allergies, asthma, or chemical sensitivities. A department in my academic library posted a sign outside the door cautioning those wearing fragrance or perfume about entering the space because strong perfumes gave one staffer migraines.

Loud, sudden noises can trigger trauma survivors, just as pleasant background music, water features, and sound machines can neutralize areas, thus rendering them pleasant. Trauma survivors are not the only group negatively affected by noises. Sometimes these issues are quite out of library workers' control. However, making our best efforts to provide neutral aural spaces is ideal.

For those calmed by taste, what is the availability of fresh, clean water and other refreshments? Most libraries offer drinking fountains, and that should suffice when it comes to providing the basics for patrons. Other types of refreshments, especially those dispensed via vending machines, are optional and may be outside of libraries' budgets. Many libraries host cafés or even restaurants in the library space, which would appeal to taste. However, what smells and sounds generated by these services are desirable or controllable? When food burns in convection or microwave ovens, how do people react to the charred odor? What noise-dampening devices do these establishments employ? Can everyone hear when smoothies are blended? What can be done about coffee grinders, expresso machines, and the steaming of milk for lattes?

Outreach and engagement activities can bring not only guests but a plethora of musicians, other performers, and even animals to the library. Concerns about patron safety around dogs, pigs, and other therapy pets are appropriate. Depending on the season, therapy animals may be taken inside libraries, or kept just outside the library building's entry doors. Assiduous attention to cleanup after animals leave the building can prevent the transmission of animal diseases, infections, and infestations to humans, as well as lessen the incidence of allergic reactions and asthma due to animal dander, saliva, and other excretions. Many patrons and library workers find the noise of animals providing pet therapy to be very loud, distracting, and alarming, especially if they have a history of trauma related to animals, and especially dogs.

INTERIOR DESIGN

Part of creating emotionally safe library environments includes the thoughtful and careful arrangement of spaces. Richardson (n.d.) suggests that individual chairs may seem unsafe to trauma survivors. Thus, rearranging the furniture is a means of creating a physically safe library environment. People suffering from PTSD monitor their environments for danger. Thus, individual chairs should border walls so that strangers cannot approach traumatized people from a vulnerable, exposed position, like from behind. Furthermore, giving patrons options to sit individually, rather than on shared sofas or other furniture, helps everyone maintain physical boundaries which support a sense of personal safety.

Other environmental considerations Richardson recommends are soothing colors for décor and paint, a neutral or pleasant aroma, and individual bathroom options. Cleanliness, signage, and welcoming interiors are ways that trauma survivors can assess library spaces. Unpleasant odors such as tobacco and urine can trigger those sensitive to smell. For those with tactile triggers, attention to sticky upholstery, inky pens, and dirty bathroom and drinking fountain fixtures is important. Given changes in library spaces over the last decades, many are not the quiet spaces where patrons have traditionally sought respite. Identifying areas as collaboration zones, quiet zones, and tech-free zones are ideas for serving the needs of all patrons.

INDOOR AIR QUALITY

Some chemicals are known to cause human disease. We're exposed to them in libraries. While tobacco smoke is the main offender, nowadays those using libraries are protected from exposure to this carcinogen. However, asbestos is often a constituent in older buildings, and is a regular threat to libraries, library staff, and library patrons. Within the last few years, the presence of asbestos temporarily closed the Glencoe Public Library (IL), the Hillman Library in Pittsburgh (PA), the Georgia Tech Library, the British Library, and the Brooklyn Public Library (NY). In 2017 an inquest determined that asbestos may have killed the Keeper of the Books at Oxford University's Bodleian Library. Professor Dennis Shaw worked there in the early 1970s. His exposure to asbestos in the workplace is believed to have led to his subsequent death from mesothelioma.

Some people experience a range of allergic reactions to carpeting, plastics, perfumes, plants, paint, or cigarette smoke. Mindfully selecting carpeting, plastics, paints, and plants with the least chemical off-gassing is critical for creating physically safe spaces for both library patrons and staff. Public and academic libraries have dealt with the well-being of their staffs by managing physical reactions to buildings that are afflicted with "sick building syndrome."

Early in 2019 ALA Council adopted the "Resolution for the Adoption of Sustainability as a Core Value of Librarianship." Given the overwhelming professional support for the idea of sustainability as a core value of librarianship, selecting environmentally sound, economically feasible, and socially equitable materials and furnishings for libraries seems an obvious practice. The careful selection of sustainable materials takes time. However, coupling trauma-informed approaches to library spaces with the idea of sustainability eases the burden for administrators or committees tasked with space renovation. Choosing sustainable materials for libraries is a sound practice because many typical or "unsustainable" materials give off strong chemical odors that patrons and workers inhale, causing headaches, nausea and upset stomach, dizziness, vomiting, and other symptoms. There are many print and online resources for creating and renovating sustainable library buildings that decision-makers may consult.

A word about plants: while some are harmful, or even poisonous to humans, the main rule of thumb about using them in public spaces is to focus on organically nurtured plants raised from organic seeds. Plants treated with pesticides should not be placed in libraries. Research by NASA identified several plants as beneficial to interior spaces because of their air-purifying capabilities. Plants are sustainable, natural alternatives to the air purifiers that many who suffer from chemical sensitivities employ within their personal spaces. The plants used in libraries can clean the air and have positive effects upon learning, productivity, efficiency, stress-reduction, pain abatement, noise pollution, and air quality. Anecdotally, the majority of university students I've welcomed into our public services office space (which is private, but publicly accessible to students who meet individually with librarians) exclaim about the presence of plants in librarians' offices and the waiting area. The students find our plants homey, inviting, and tranquil. However, this may not be the case with trauma survivors, so you should tread carefully when it comes to placing plants in libraries.

BUILDING MAINTENANCE

Some problems with building maintenance may be out of the library administration's control. Anecdotally, my library's roof developed leaks in 2012, and this problem went unaddressed until we got a new roof in the summer of 2018. As a state institution, getting on the capital improvements list was the first step in remedying the problem. Then having the leaks categorized as an emergent need landed the library's roof replacement nearer the top of the list. Due to the leaks, the library's fourth floor was a mess. By 2014 we had covered the books and stacks there with waterproof plastic sheeting to protect them from leaks. Ceiling tiles were removed as they became saturated and stained. Trash bins and five-gallon containers dotted the floor as collection sites for rainwater and to protect the carpet from water damage. Our students shared photos of the damage and disarray on social media.

All of us were concerned about the state of our printed materials, but some of us were also concerned about the environmental health implications of the constant dampness, and the potential for mold and mildew spores to affect student and staff health. The carpeting was never replaced on that floor, so there's no telling what students studying up there and browsing the stacks might be inhaling. Moreover, how would parents feel about their college student's constant exposure to standing water and water damage over the short or long term?

NEUTRAL SPACES

Bath (2008) shares evidence that the creation of trauma-informed environments is crucial for therapeutic alteration. So while providing therapeutic environments does not fall within our scope as librarians, we can align our spaces with trauma-informed principles so that, at the least, they are neutral and do not actively trigger PTSD responses. Mindful attention to the built library environment should include efforts at neutralizing the space for all those who spend time within it.

Trauma-informed approaches to staff appearance should include good hygiene, professional attire, name tags or other means of easily identifying staff, modest clothing that does not sexually provoke, and discreet jewelry that does not promote religious faith. Regarding the smell of tobacco smoke, people working in libraries using a trauma-informed approach to customer services should minimize the odor of cigarette smoke on their person, lest the odor give someone a headache or trigger re-traumatization. Liberal use of chewing gum, mouthwash, or lightly scented lotions or scented hand-sanitizers on the hands can dissipate the smoky smell. Having smokers spray their clothing with an odor-eliminating product that is also scentless helps library workers offering trauma-informed customer services.

Undoubtedly, the people who work in libraries are just as affected by the physical and sensory environment in which they spend their workday as patrons are. Flocos (2014) pays detailed attention to the built environment and its effect on workers. She implies that views of nature throughout the workday may have curative influences. Other improvements to the workplace she recommends are green practices that increase productivity. External noise-reduction is crucial, especially in regard to children's spaces. Flocos cites a study of children at two schools, one adjacent to an airport and the other nowhere near an airport. She concludes that reading comprehension skills and the long-term memory of children near the old airport improved once air traffic moved to the new airport, while the performance of children near the new airport declined.

SPECIAL CONSIDERATIONS FOR CHILDREN

In creating safe environments for children, the library administration and staff should be guided by several principles: consistency, reliability, predictability, availability, honesty, and transparency. Having consistent hours and consistent staffing is essential. Children rely on librarians and library staff being available to help them while they're in the library. Sometimes, in fact, a school or public librarian may be the only stable and predictable adult in a child's life. Research shows that the one thing above all that has positive outcomes in traumatized children's lives is adults who care for and love the child. Sometimes that level of care and love is just not available in the child's home. Offering comfort, support, and encouragement to children who use our library services, spaces, and collections is not a trivial job duty: it is vitally important. Many librarians may never know the effect they have on a child's development and growth into a successful adult. Anglin and Sachs (2003) remarked that controlling and punitive responses by adults create unsafe environments for both children and adults with high ACEs. You should remove signs about rules and punishment from areas serving children, and instead reframe the language around what kinds of behaviors you want to encourage. Eradicating library fines and fees is especially important for children. The inability to use library materials because of their or their parents' lack of economic means presents real barriers to access to information that might inform young people and also offer them a respite from traumatic realities.

CONFLICT IN FREE SPEECH

Another barrier to entering academic libraries is expressions of dissent and free speech. At my campus, East Tennessee State University (ETSU), the plaza in front of the Sherrod Library is identified as a free speech zone. There are other, less traveled zones on campus, but given the plaza's central location, internal and external groups choose this space in which to demonstrate, table and hand out literature, and preach.

On September 28, 2016, ETSU made national news when a student wearing a gorilla mask, Tristan Rettke, taunted peaceful Black Lives Matter students who were demonstrating on the plaza in front of the Sherrod Library. In a show of solidarity, more than 100 students, staff, and faculty joined the Black Lives Matter group the next day, again in front of the library. There was a quick response by the administration in support of the demonstrating students and the man in the gorilla mask was arrested, removed, and charged with a felony civil rights intimidation. He was indicted in March 2017 by a grand jury. Ironically, a fountain commemorating the desegregation of ETSU in 1966 is prominently centered in the plaza. The names of each of those persons of color who were the first to enroll at ETSU are displayed around the fountain's sides.

This space in front of the Sherrod Library is used for various internal campus events like Welcome Week, a community showcase (in which local businesses ply students with swag), voter registration, and even library events, like a celebration of William Shakespeare's birthday. External groups use this space as well, but they must register with the university's facilities reservationist who handles the student center and surrounding grounds. There are other spaces available on campus, but visitors prefer the space in front of the library on account of its high traffic and its visibility to the student body. Currently, ETSU faces lawsuits from four preachers who say their free speech rights were violated by the university for a variety of reasons. When preachers come to campus, they express their views to every passerby on the plaza. Members of the Gideon's and Jehovah's Witnesses station themselves on the plaza in order to share their literature with the students.

As tenants in the building, we have no say over how the space in front of the library is used, even though the preachers' use of the space presents clear barriers to accessing the building and thus our services, programs, and collections. The noise generated outside the building makes working, studying, concentrating, and focusing on productive activities nearly impossible. The noises include loud music, singing, chanting, protesting, and amplified ranting from preachers whose audio PA systems can be clearly heard inside the library. Moreover, our library management group is concerned that events happening in front of the library may be perceived as being endorsed by the library, when this is rarely the case.

Some students at ETSU have complained about preachers who verbally attack them as they walk between campus buildings. In September 2014, the traveling street preacher Ross Jackson told a student she looked like she weighed as much as a football linebacker. Some of the preachers regularly yell and taunt students, especially women, who wear their hair short and dress "immodestly" in yoga pants, shorts, and dresses and skirts above the knee.

Having the free speech zone in front of the Sherrod Library is both good and bad. When these contentious events happen, we have an opportunity to model free speech and intellectual freedom, and to support and commend those who exercise those rights at our front steps. Yet, this boon has also brought access problems to light. When students gather to listen to or counter the preachers, they fill in the steps leading to the library's only public entrance. People who have survived religious abuse are easily triggered when preachers yell scripture, or tell the young women wearing shorts in public they're going to hell or vocalize their hatred of LGBTQ people.

Some international students are especially leery of these outpourings and avoid the library during the eight or ten hours that these preachers occupy the plaza. But these outbursts affect our native-born students as well. They feel unsafe, condemned, and harassed.

Students have asked the university administration to limit the preachers' access to campus or move them to a more isolated place so that their free speech rights are acknowledged, but they will have less traumatic effects upon the student body. Students regularly show empathy for each other and want to protect those suffering from PTSD, specifically our military veteran population, from re-traumatization. Some students use back-channel methods like sending Twitter, Snapchat, and Instagram posts to warn their fellow students away from the library on days when the preachers are active.

Both faculty and students have expressed dismay and frustration at being exposed to the larger-than-life images that anti-abortion groups present while tabling on the plaza in front of the library. The students have been even more vocal in expressing their displeasure with preachers who travel the campus circuit as part of their lawsuit-generating agenda. A cartoon appeared in a spring 2017 issue of the *East Tennessean,* ETSU's student newspaper, expressing the frustration of walking through a gauntlet of offensive visual and auditory stimuli. But the university's location in the Southeast makes this type of situation almost inevitable, since it is in the heart of the Bible Belt.

PART II

The Six Guiding Principles of Trauma-Informed Approaches

5

Safety

The first pillar, or principle, of trauma-informed care is safety. Therefore, everyone, including workers, community members, and visitors, should feel physically, psychologically, and culturally safe.

Creating a culture of safety relies on tangible changes we can make to the environment that are easy to evaluate and easy to measure. Focusing on physical safety is the place to begin, because when everyone feels physically safe, the other types of safety can expand from this baseline infrastructure.

PHYSICAL SAFETY

Libraries have always recognized the value of physical safety for objects and sometimes for people as well. We lock the library's front doors when there are no services offered. We lock our doors, drawers, and filing cabinets when we leave our offices. Rare and special books and collections are safeguarded by special access to collections and special handling procedures, such as limiting patrons to the use of pencils and enforcing protocols for handling valuable or fragile books. Many libraries have security measures in place, including identifiable staff who monitor access to the building and the behavior that takes place within it as well.

Sadly, our traditional focus on keeping collection items safe has created a culture of rigidity and regulations, and a stereotype of librarians as gate-keepers whose first response is "no." Library spaces feel like prisons to some patrons. While the structure, order, and routine common in library operations may appeal to some individuals, they are more likely to trigger negative responses in trauma survivors. In fact, Amy Edmondson (2018), an expert on psychological safety in the workplace and a professor at the Harvard Business School, says that organizations are usually designed in ways that exacerbate rather than ameliorate our natural tendencies for self-protection. She cites the organization's hierarchical structure as the main source for creating and maintaining status differences.

Feelings of safety require that our physical well-being is unthreatened. Within the library building, patrons expect to be free from destructive behavior, physical or sexual attacks, substance abuse, toxins, weapons, aggression, coercion, threats, lack of control, and so on. According to Bloom (2000), physically safe spaces, including libraries, provide a model for supportive and caring relationships.

Weapons, particularly handguns, are problematic for libraries, as the number of active shooter incidents rises in our public schools, universities, churches, festivals, and other community spaces. Most public and K–12 libraries are protected by state and federal laws and may display signs on their entrance doors banning concealed and unconcealed weapons. Some Americans believe that the presence of guns in libraries may deter violence, while others believe that guns should be regulated on public library property. Federal law bans firearms in K–12 school buildings under the Gun-Free School Zones Act of 1990. The conditions at university and college campuses are murkier, however. Arkansas and Georgia allow students and faculty to carry guns on campus, and Tennessee and Texas both permit "concealed carry" on their campuses under certain conditions. Some university systems have defied the state law's authority, however, by banning firearms from their campuses or from specific buildings.

As in all supportive and caring relationships, library workers should employ noncoercive forms of persuasion with patrons. The behaviors modeled and accepted within the organization should be both healthy and safe. Workers should be committed to nonviolence to others and to nonviolent means of conflict resolution. That said, there is still room for a healthy expression of assertiveness sometimes.

All of these components create a safe space that ensures success. Aside from the actions taken to ensure the safety of all, another thing to consider is the internal baggage associated with certain spaces. When library staff experience bullying or emotional distress from supervisors gaslighting them, or any behaviors associated with toxic environments, those negative experiences remain in certain spaces. While I'm not suggesting that these spaces should be cleared regularly by burning sage and banishing the negative energy, what I am saying is that care should be taken in choosing the spaces in which people meet. Some spaces, like meeting rooms, are more neutral than others. But the ones "owned" by the bullies who steamroll staff should be avoided. Likewise, you should schedule meetings in spaces where the meeting is the only way that area is used for the span of the meeting. Sometimes meeting spaces double as staff kitchen areas, workspaces, or training spaces. Ensuring that meetings are confidential and remain uninterrupted goes without saying. But when you have library staff popping in to nuke their ramen or pizza rolls or wash their lunch dishes, this creates unneeded intrusions and distractions and is disrespectful to those in attendance at a meeting. While these types of interruptions may indicate a loose, informal, hip workplace culture, they also demonstrate the meeting convener's lack of emotional and professional intelligence. They also display an underlying lack of respect on the convener's part for their coworkers' time and attention.

Empowering the library staff by including safety training within their professional development is sensible. Libraries of all types occasionally have to respond to situations that compromise the safety of the building, of patrons, or of those working therein. Having automated external defibrillators (AEDs) within libraries is quite common. Having these devices on-site can save lives, and training library staff to use them helps maintain a safe library environment. Having time to run the library staff through disaster scenarios is uncommon, but it can help create preparedness in case of active shooters, hurricanes, tornadoes, fires, and all manner of natural and man-made disasters that could affect the safety and well-being of our patrons and ourselves. In 2016 our library staff participated in a staff training in which campus public safety officers trained everyone in how to shelter in place due to weather threats, hazardous material threats, active shooters, and armed assault or hostage situations on campus. Our library has always been a designated shelter for tornadoes, but it now also serves as a refuge from active shooters. In August 2018, just a few days into the fall semester, ETSU's campus was locked down because of an altercation between contractors on campus, wherein a firearm was reported. While we inside the library were safe and understood the safety protocol, students new to campus were either panicked or clueless about the threat.

Keeping everyone safe from needle sticks and overdosing is another avenue for providing safety inside the library. Public libraries in many urban areas have to deal with discarded needles used for illegal and legal purposes, patrons overdosing, and other related self-harm activities. Libraries have struggled in their efforts to cope with these issues. Usually the first response is to limit patrons' access to bathrooms in order to deter self-harm behaviors. Some libraries have installed blue lights in their bathrooms because this color of lighting makes it more difficult for IV drug users to see well enough to find a vein. Increased monitoring of the bathrooms is a common suggestion, and some security experts have called for video surveillance as a deterrent. However, living in a surveillance state may trigger many who want to avoid cameras simply for privacy reasons. Installing sharps containers in library bathrooms can mitigate the needle stick accidents that other library patrons or the library's housekeeping staff may experience. Additionally, some libraries keep a supply of Narcan, either the injection or the nasal spray, on-site and administer it to those who are exhibiting overdose symptoms. Narcan is the brand name of naloxone, a medication that reverses the effects of opioid overdose by blocking the effects of opioids in the brain.

In late December 2019, Chinese authorities identified a novel coronavirus (COVID-19) that was isolated on January 7, 2020. The first cases were reported in the United States and confirmed on January 20, 2020. As it spread effecting regions unequally, the federal and, later, state governments had provided guidelines for social distancing measures. By March 11, the World Health Organization had declared the COVID-19 outbreak a pandemic. In response to the outbreak, several cities and states issued stay-at-home orders, requiring a majority of school, special, public, and academic libraries to close their buildings in an effort to flatten the curve of infection so that hospitals were not overwhelmed by multiple COVID-19 cases. As experts learned more about COVID-19's spread, libraries were problematic spaces because the greatest risks came from places where, as Natalie Dean, a biostatistics professor at the University of Florida, said, "people are in close proximity indoors for extended periods of time" (Lopez 2020).

State and federal guidelines for early phases of opening recommend that businesses offering personal surfaces remove books, magazines, and other items on which the virus can survive several days. The meaning of personal safety in libraries, and in the world, is different now. How the safety of library staff and patrons is safeguarded remains to be seen. Some ideas include exposing physical materials to UV lights or keeping them quarantined between borrowers for several days. Public service areas may install plexiglass between library staff and patrons, a practice that essential businesses remaining open during stay-at-home orders instituted to promote physical distancing. Many library staff may wear masks and require that people using the library wear them as a condition for entry to the building.

There is a divide between library workers and library administration and other stakeholders who have differing priorities. Administration and stakeholders want libraries to return to business as usual, as they claim libraries are essential to communities and thus, must be one of the first organizations to reopen. Fobazi Ettarh's ideas about vocational awe play into this dynamic. Ettarh describes this as "librarians are working to save the democratic values of society as well as going above and beyond to serve the needs of their neighbors and communities" (Ettarh 2018). Library workers' main concern is maintaining everyone's physical safety.

PSYCHOLOGICAL SAFETY OF PATRONS

After attending to the physical safety of the library workplace, administrators should examine the psychological safety felt by two groups: patrons and staff. Psychological safety is compromised by a range of behaviors that includes sarcasm, condescension, public humiliation, negative tones of voice and body language, inconsistent rules, procedures, and policies, favoritism, infantilizing, gaslighting, shaming, and blaming, among others. People who grew up around these behaviors as part of their ACEs are easily triggered by exposure to them in libraries' customer service operations.

The rule of thumb here is to flip the Golden Rule, which says that we should treat everyone the same way we would like to be treated. Good, right? Well, in some cases, this is not so good. We all start at different levels due to what we learned from our families of origin. So while all families have their own specific form of dysfunction, some are much more functional than others. For example, if you appreciate efficiency and brevity, that is how you will treat others. However, these types of interactions can seem robotic, perfunctory, and dismissive to some patrons. So when dealing with trauma survivors, you should *treat others the way they'd like to be treated*. This presents difficulties, however.

Libraries struggle to be all things to all people. Library workers must maintain their personal integrity and authenticity. This doesn't mean that one should change oneself in order to fit everyone's expectations. However, library workers are accustomed to and are, in fact, very attuned to reading people. Much like servers do in the hospitality industry, we can tell, from the get-go, whether someone is in a hurry and wants efficiency, or if someone seeks a slower, more relational interaction with us. And we adjust accordingly. This is emotional labor. We all do it to some extent, whether on the clock or at home. Those of us who work in customer services are adept at providing an experience that the patron wants, or that the administration expects according to our brand, regardless of how we personally feel at the moment.

Everyone benefits when libraries' customer service approaches model trust, consistency, and continuity. For patrons who have experienced the sudden loss of a parent or caregiver, having library staff abruptly depart from an interaction without explanation can trigger similar feelings of overwhelming anguish from their past. And interrupting patrons does not make them feel safe; they can feel judged, or blamed, or inconsequential.

Library procedures should make everyone feel culturally safe. Cultural safety recognizes and respects the cultural differences between library workers and patrons and sets up a dynamic in which everyone's needs, expectations, and rights are met. When we work with people from differing backgrounds, our procedures should not diminish, demean, or disempower our patrons, or our colleagues. The library administration should recognize and avoid stereotypical barriers and understand how culture shock influences both patrons and library workers.

Minimizing power differentials when dealing with patrons or other library workers is the first step. This entails working with the person in an open, authentic manner and facilitating the process of communication. This does not mean telling the patron that they need these two peer-reviewed articles or telling them what they really should be looking for. It is being open to where the information relationship leads. As library workers, it is our responsibility to negotiate and change service models on the fly in order to provide the service that the patron needs. Otherwise, our service models can easily alienate patrons from the library. We should let our patrons make decisions, but we should also be firm about restricting the time spent in this way, especially if the patrons are working toward a deadline. A brief conversation lets everyone learn about each other, share goals and understanding, and ease into the relationship. Calling this a relationship rather than a transaction is culturally safe. Who wants to be considered a transaction? That mode of thinking is over.

Nicola Andrews (2018) compares our Western thinking about research, which is transactional, to the Kaupapa Maori model, in which conducting research requires forming relationships and consulting with elders in the community first. Being culturally responsive requires self-reflection and intellectual preparation on the part of library workers. Learning the history of the communities we serve and thinking about our own personal histories and how those two experiences are different and similar can help us add a culturally responsive component to our customer service.

Understanding librarianship's history with marginalized groups provides insight into why many groups and individuals feel reluctant about using our services. Also, understanding how your institution and other local library systems historically and currently serve and interact with cultural communities can provide micro-level insights into ongoing challenges. Safe relationships are ones that are consistent, predictable, respectful, nonviolent, non-shaming, and non-blaming.

Maintaining neutrality about a patron's ideas and perspectives as they express them in the reference interview or transaction is important. Adding stock phrases such as "Is that so?" "I've never thought about that in this way before," or similar phrasing can neutralize the exchange. This doesn't mean that library workers should be flip or robotic and simply spout canned phrases. Being authentic in the moment creates engagement and interest. However, having three or four neutral sentences in your mind ahead of time to draw upon helps when you are stymied in responding to a patron's beliefs or opinions. Using a stock phrase here and there may give you enough time to deliver meaningful and empathetic words that satisfy the patron's underlying information need. Some questions and phrases that you should use with patrons and coworkers are: "What can I do to help?" "I trust your decision," "What can I do differently?" and "What do you think is the best course of action?" Granted, these are highly situational and removed from the original context. But librarians already routinely ask the first question, "What can I do to help?"

The remaining three can occur anywhere in a one-on-one situation at a service desk, in a reference interview, or at a meeting.

Granted, psychological safety can take much work on the survivors' part, and they must rely on themselves to self-protect against triggering. They can erect strong boundaries and keep themselves out of harm's way or leave difficult situations immediately and use their skills to calm themselves. But as libraries providing trauma-informed customer service, it is our responsibility to set up our patrons for success when they interact with us. For trauma survivors, being psychologically safe means that they feel comfortable with interpersonal risk-taking. Essentially, feeling comfortable is about trusting the library and trusting the people who are trying to satisfy your informational needs.

PSYCHOLOGICAL SAFETY OF LIBRARY WORKERS

Paul Santagata, the head of industry at Google, revealed that a two-year study on team performance concluded that the highest-performing teams all have one thing in common—a sense of psychological safety (Delizonna 2017). This means that workers won't be punished when they make mistakes or speak their mind, or be creative, or otherwise stick their necks out. Asking library workers how psychologically safe they feel and what steps can be taken to increase those feelings, if they're low, should happen regularly as a part of an assessment culture.

Amy Edmondson's tool "Team Learning and Psychological Safety Survey" is a 24-item measure that can help libraries assess their psychological safety climate, at least from their workers' perspective, and then act accordingly. Edmonson, who wrote *The Fearless Organization: Creating Psychological Safety in the Workplace for Learning, Innovation, and Growth* (2018), says that psychological safety in the workplace is not the norm. Library workers who feel psychologically unsafe don't bring their whole selves into the library each day. They hide behind a mask of perfection that requires high levels of emotional energy and labor to sustain. They can't express their creativity. They self-censor their skills and talents. Such self-silencing limits workers' ability to learn on the job.

The answers to the questions below can help you gauge the safety of your organization's culture, and more specifically, the division or unit in which you work with others to meet the library's objectives.

- How comfortable do people feel in team meetings about things they don't know?
- Do they ask questions or maintain a façade of knowing?
- How openly and frequently is information shared?
- How comfortable do people feel about raising concerns, reservations, or conversing about difficult topics within the team environment?

- How is criticism of "the way things are done here" dealt with by other team members and the administration?
- How are open questioning and challenges to the established order received?
- How often do library workers admit that they are wrong or sorry for mistakes or poor decision-making?
- How defensive are people whose decisions are questioned?
- Do conversations about business as usual take place in public, or behind the scenes, with only one of two people making decisions?
- How does the library deal with mistakes, failures, and critical incidents? Do library workers distance themselves so they are not blamed? Or are these situations seen as an opportunity for team building and team learning?
- How often do people give and receive feedback? Are outsiders from other teams giving and taking feedback? Are all team members invited to participate irrespective of their rank, role, or job title?
- How prevalent are power inequalities based on age, seniority in role, gender, race, ability, gender identity, and so on?
- On a personal/professional level, how does the library value and use your skills and talents? Are you encouraged to participate in all areas, or are you expected to remain strictly inside the parameters of your job description? Must you ask permission to work in other areas and learn new aspects of the library's operations as a whole?
- When have you felt that your contributions and efforts were compromised by your colleagues?
- How often do people ask each other for help?
- How comfortable are people with disagreement and dissent in team meetings?
- What do you know about your colleagues' lives outside the workplace?

Answering these questions give a sense of the functional level of the library team, and of your organization. Those insights can help library workers determine the next steps to take, such as speaking with a supervisor about how the library can become more transparent in its decision-making, become more open to exploring new ideas, and become more agile in responding to calls for new service models, collections, and so on. After becoming familiar with the level of psychological safety in the library, workers can either reconcile themselves to their place in the system and fortify themselves for the daily grind, or work toward creating meaningful change that benefits all who work within the space. Or, alternatively, they may seek work elsewhere and ask pointed questions in interviews as a way to find work in a safer library organizational climate and culture.

Libraries should foster and cultivate psychological safety with their staff because ensuring staff well-being and job satisfaction is one of the most basic obligations an employer has to its workers. In other words, it's the right and ethical thing to do. Moreover, psychological safety makes good business sense. It positively correlates with objective and subjective indicators of team performance. It positively correlates with the faster adoption of new technologies and the development of innovative products, faster adaptation to new market circumstances, increased customer satisfaction, and the earlier identification of potential risks to operations. In the end, psychological safety positively affects the bottom line.

Tips for creating a psychologically safe workplace include leading by example, encouraging active listening, and cultivating an open and receptive mindset. For example, imagine that a senior administrator set a very poor example for their staff. The person routinely bullied and condescended to everyone, but specifically one tenure-track librarian. Given the administrator's regular dismissive tone, their direct reports' behavior toward the scapegoated librarian grew worse and mimicked their harshness. This could create an ongoing lack of psychological safety in meetings where those personalities were present. Feeling unsafe closes conversations. Others sensitive to bullying put up walls and fortified their boundaries. The results may be a culture of silence in meetings, in which a senior administrator felt compelled to stage-direct everyone in attendance and prompt them to speak up and report on their areas' functions. Understandably, the staff and faculty at a library experiencing these behaviors may still feel shy about making themselves vulnerable to embarrassment or punishment by asking questions or offering new ideas, despite having some staff and faculty turnover as well as a new person leading who models and demonstrates fairness in their leadership. Let's imagine that the senior-level administrator mentioned at the beginning of the paragraph never admitted to making mistakes, nor did this individual respond with appreciation when staff approached them with input that doesn't mirror their agenda and worldview. They are unable to acknowledge that all the breakdowns of systems, processes, and collegial relationships within the library are due to their decision-making. Nor do they ask for feedback. This example of a psychologically unsafe workplace provides examples of what not to do. It illustrates the importance of creating a positive organizational culture where everyone is valued, heard, respected, and treated with dignity.

Part of active listening includes mirroring what someone says to you by saying something like, "It sounds like you're saying that the maps collection cannot be deaccessioned in a years' time, is that right?" A back-and-forth of this type gets everyone to a consensus on their understanding of the matter under discussion. Asking people who rarely speak in meetings to express their opinions can bring in others who may be reluctant to share their perspective. Providing everyone with the tools to succeed as a team can only help the long-term functioning of the organization. So, sharing feedback is important. Instructing people on how to share their feedback is also important. Giving everyone the tools and strategies for conveying helpful feedback takes professional development, as does helping everyone see that feedback is a way to strengthen ideas and processes, not a means for cutting off someone at the knees.

Jake Herway (2017), writing for Gallup.com, recommends that groups gather and answer four questions which are designed to promote a culture of psychological safety. They are:

1. What can we count on each other for?
2. What is our team's purpose?
3. What is the reputation we aspire to have?
4. What do we need to do differently to achieve that reputation and fulfill our purpose?

Herway stresses that the order of these questions is as important as the questions themselves. He uses a round-robin and asks specific workers, "What can we count on you for?" One might answer "I always make my deadlines; you can count on me." And this provides an opportunity for coworkers to talk about when the person on the spot delivered on time, and it also gives an opportunity for someone else to speak up about the person's other high-value skills that are highly regarded by the team. This helps everyone feel validated and secure, and helps individuals feel less isolated and unappreciated by their team or leadership. Along these same lines, using a similar process for annual reviews can help in the areas of accountability and transparency. The 360-degree feedback model takes into account feedback from an employee's assistants, colleagues, and supervisors. This type of model can help identify areas where communication and trust between library workers break down, and it can help with conflict resolution, if that is the root cause of dysfunctionality in the workplace.

Unlike the toxic conflicts I've described in earlier paragraphs, healthy conflict offers a means of creating psychological safety for library workers. Asking questions and cultivating curiosity are good tools for encouraging healthy conflict. Debating ideas and discussing their positive, negative, and neutral values provides so many more opportunities—for growth, for understanding, for collegiality—than judging and throwing out ideas does. Libraries can miss out on a lot of potentially transformative opportunities because they lack the tools for managing healthy conflict. Instead, many libraries function, or barely function, because everyone is primed to avoid conflict. If we are to believe the stereotypes about people working in libraries, we remain quiet, we don't ruffle feathers, and we avoid direct confrontation. But passive-aggressive feelings (and actions) can still exist beneath the surface.

SOCIAL SAFETY

Social safety means feeling safe with other people in group, public, or private settings. It means feeling secure. We are cared for and trusted. We can express our deepest thoughts and feelings and our social network responds with empathy. We aren't afraid of being abandoned, isolated, or misjudged. We are unencumbered by pressures associated with the competition for scarce resources. We are intellectually and professionally stimulated. Most organizations are set up to reward competition, efficiency, and other values characteristic of capitalist settings. Many libraries are not organized to maximize the human potential for growth.

Interpersonal relationships are difficult for trauma survivors. That includes most of us. Trusting others is difficult and may be impossible for those with the highest ACEs scores. Those of us who are employed in toxic work environments experience the library workplace as dangerous, duplicitous, and ultimately, a site for professional betrayal. Whether we are a library patron or new library staffer, when our experiences caution us to be careful and keep boundaries in place, we suspect kindness as someone trying to get one over on us and our minds race a dozen steps ahead, prepping for the long game exemplified by humiliation, shame, blame, and reprisals. When we expect that people will violate our boundaries, many flip the dynamic and bulldoze through others' boundaries first as a preemptive strategy. The social skills for patrons and staff in this group are poor or impaired, and their ability to communicate clearly and meaningfully is hampered. In library teams, persons with power, such as supervisors, can twist the organizational climate and culture into one in which their bullying is accepted as the norm. Bullies seek to replay their childhood experiences, but with them as the bully instead of the victim. Placing injured, dysfunctional personalities in charge of others presents a very real barrier for operational, psychological, and social safety within the library workplace. Christopher Freeze (n.d.) writes about workplace violence and how childhood trauma can contribute to it: children whose neurodevelopment was damaged by abuse and chaos can only replicate those dynamics in their personal and professional lives as adults.

In his book *Reboot: Leadership and the Art of Growing Up* (2019), Jerry Colonna approaches his leadership coaching by acknowledging this dynamic in venture capitalists and C-suite executives (chief financial officer, chief operating officer, chief information officer, chief technology officer, etc.). But performing radical self-inquiry can help leaders realize how their childhood and family baggage directly sabotages their effectiveness in both their personal and professional lives. Colonna says that the power wielded by leaders who are unwilling to self-reflect can perpetuate a climate of hidden or overt violence in the workplace. Ultimately, he tries to make his clients realize how changing their relationships with others and examining their beliefs about themselves can carry them into greater effectiveness.

The questions we ask to determine the level of social safety in our workplace are quite similar to the ones we ask about psychological safety:

- Do people only advocate for their own views?

- Do library workers blame others for problems, or do they examine problems within the organizational context?
- Do people assume that the only perspective that is valuable is their own?
- Do people inquire about different perspectives?
- How open or closed are library workers to talking about the differences and similarities between people's points of view?
- How genuine is their interest in innovating for future services, collections, and programming?

Socially safe environments are completely free from abusive relationships, power dynamics, and feelings of isolation. A sense of connection and connectedness pervades. Library workers don't feel isolated, scapegoated, or excluded from sharing their opinions in the context of improving overall operations. Both patrons and library workers are relaxed and easygoing. Emotional intelligence is high and is evident in all decision-making and service models. The tolerance for individualism is great, especially since libraries of all types typically attract the unconventional, either as workers or patrons. Socially protected libraries share a belief in being and feeling safe. Tolerance, and even acceptance, of individual eccentricity is abundant, as long as the idiosyncrasies are not harmful to others. The awareness of personal, interpersonal, and group dynamics is paramount in socially safe organizations. Library workers and patrons see emotional and social abuses and understand how to name them and change them.

MORAL SAFETY

The last component comprising a safety context is moral safety. Creating a library environment, or organization of any type, that is suffused by moral safety may be challenging. Though closely associated with religion, morality comes down to the basics of what is right and what is wrong in situations and in dealing with people. Morality stems from universal systems of values and principles of conduct. Some of those codes are covered by etiquette, some by law, and some by religion.

White Christian evangelicals tend to overlook President Donald Trump's infidelities, multiple marriages, dishonesty, disparaging rhetoric toward immigrants, refugees, and LGBTQ people, and multiple incidents of sexual misconduct because he supports their traditional mindsets through his rhetoric and policies. The notion of morality in the twenty-first century is at question. According to a 2011 poll, 60 percent of white evangelicals said that public officials who commit immoral acts in their personal life cannot behave ethically in their public and professional lives. But five years later, 72 percent of white evangelicals did assert that an elected official who commits immoral acts in his personal life could still behave ethically in his professional life. This sea change seems to directly reflect the example and influence of President Trump.

Given the ambiguity characterizing morality of late, the library administration can and should take the high ground, operate ethically, and do what it can to counter the current negative trends in politics and business. However, this presents difficulties, since many libraries adopt business models and performance measures informed by terms like *efficiency* and *return on investment*, and thus move away from human services models and the examples set by nonprofit organizations. Certainly, libraries can leave morals at the door and divorce them from their everyday operations, but this doesn't align with our professional Code of Ethics, or with trauma-informed approaches to library customer service. It's likely that many library administrators fall somewhere in between these two paradigms. A frequent problem for library directors and deans is that they must try to satisfy the interests of three different parties: the staff, the stakeholders, and the community. This requires sacrifices and compromises with those who hold the purse strings, such as city governments and college presidents, who have the final say in library decision-making. Another example of divided interests is library closures and reopenings during the 2020 coronavirus pandemic.

Moral distress lies in knowing what the right thing to do is but being constrained by external forces from following that path. Acting in ways that contradict our personal beliefs and values while we're in the library can create stress, anxiety, and frustration, and it can imbue library staff with feelings of hypocrisy, or hopelessness about meaningful change in the future. Library workers distressed by the lack of morals they encounter in the workplace can become seriously depressed or discouraged by spending time in organizations whose questionable values do not reflect their own—these organizations decide between business as usual and the lives of library workers.

In a morally safe environment, library workers complete their tasks, serve others, and interact collegially because their sense of rightness and fairness is supported by the institution and by their supervisors. But in a morally unsafe environment, the administration's actions often don't adhere to the library's stated vision, mission, or values. What is the point of paying lip service to a transparent assessment of services, collections, and programs that never happens? How can a workplace that doesn't learn from failure nurture the creativity of its leaders and staff? Where is the civility in practice that is enunciated in the library's formally stated values? Where is the accountability mentioned in our statement on creating a library of excellence? Where do those high ethical standards of honesty and fairness occur, if not within our own library workplaces?

Our library patrons recovering from traumatic childhood experiences were abused because of corrupt family and institutional power dynamics. When our libraries replicate these abuses of institutional and systemic power, we fail to function morally. Creating morally safe libraries where patrons and library workers find respite from toxic, punitive environments is one way to stop the cycle from repeating itself. Morally compromised organizations confirm for trauma survivors that their abusers were correct, and that abuse is normative. Learning the difference between right and wrong is, for some, an ongoing lifelong lesson. Moral intelligence is compromised by those who model exploitation, manipulation, bad behavior, and poor conduct. Doing the right thing at the right moment isn't just rational; evidence exists that managers with high moral intelligence are also very effective at their jobs. Moral library leaders function with high integrity and high levels of responsibility, compassion, and forgiveness.

CONCLUSION

Libraries that are committed to actively working within a trauma-informed framework should consider the various levels of safety present in their buildings. They should examine both their spoken and unspoken practices and beliefs. They should note the unwritten "understandings" that inform much decision-making and bring them to light, or actively counteract them with written policies and guidelines that will raise the level of safety for staff and patrons alike. Library administrators can and should actively change aspects of the library to align with these domains of physical safety, psychological safety, social safety, and moral safety.

6

Trustworthiness and Transparency

O vercoming trauma survivors' institutional mistrust can be difficult. Library anxiety is a dynamic we're familiar with, and it can stop patrons in their tracks upon entering the building. No doubt many library users appreciate our online collection and remote services like e-mail and chat. Those models let them avoid physically visiting a space that they may not trust based on earlier negative experiences. Trustworthiness and transparency are two ideals that the trauma-informed library exemplifies. These encompass instilling a sense of safety in patrons and the library staff, which was outlined in the preceding chapter. Trustworthiness boils down to our actions matching our words, values, and beliefs. Building trust begins with establishing and maintaining credibility, reliability, and intimacy.

Safety and trust are not the same, but they align together nicely when both are intentionally implemented within the library. Transparency invites and welcomes patrons inside the organization, allowing them to see aspects of our work that are normally hidden. Transparency engenders trust. At some level, we're familiar and comfortable with citing our sources when it comes to writing papers, so organizational transparency pushes our practices a bit further to show our work. This practice gives patrons insight into how our library's infrastructure came to be and what forces influenced its creation. Furthermore, our priorities and agendas should be shared, not kept secret or put into play by one person behind the scenes who is moving chess pieces around the board arbitrarily.

TRANSPARENCY

Trauma-informed and responsive libraries exemplify trust and transparency by modeling these values via their actions. The library's statement of its values is public, whether on the website or available in print form in the building, where everyone can discern what agenda guides our decision-making and spending and service models. Publicly correcting our mistakes helps to hold our organization accountable for poor decision-making. Instead of sending in a clean-up crew to cover tracks and erase mistakes, libraries should own up to lapses and failures when they occur and improve their operations by learning from these negative outcomes.

Trauma-informed and trauma-responsive libraries should try to conduct all their business transparently. The library's procedures should be written in plain, inclusive language that is vetted for triggers. Organizational processes like strategic planning, assigning tasks to individuals, and refining or creating new service models should be explained in appropriate language, and trauma survivors should be involved in those tasks at all levels.

Budgets should be shared publicly so that patrons understand the cost of the services, collections, and programs that the library offers. Correspondingly, budgets should be shared internally as well, so that library staff understand how the money is apportioned and why. Lack of transparency around money and spending can generate animosity among library workers when they don't understand why money can be found for electronic resources but not for personnel, programming, or outreach. The lack of parity between departments often needs either explanation or rectification.

Many libraries operate within a scarcity model. Amy Fifarek (2014) writes that scarcity is part of our mythos and reality as librarians. The word *scarcity* holds different meanings and experiences, depending on the library in which it occurs. In Appalachia, we have a pervasive poverty mindset that informs all budgetary decisions. The last time our library's print collections were robust was in the 1980s. Each year our databases and resources, which were never abundant, are cut. Such prolonged scarcity affects morale and mindsets. It affects the ability to function and results in a multitude of short-term fixes that never solve problems but create larger intractable ones in their wake. Library administrators can move money from some budget lines, but not others. Transparency with budgeting makes the assumptions and rationale for decisions clear. It is essential to organization-wide trust.

One example of this is the preponderance of "techno-chauvinism" in libraries, which I believe is due to our scarcity mindset. Many librarians assume that technology has the answers to all our problems. For short-term thinking and fixes, investing in software is cheaper than hiring a person who must receive pay and benefits. Techno-chauvinists value algorithms over human judgment, skill, and interactions. They fetishize apps and platforms like BrowZine, which present more barriers than actual access to locating an organization's academic journals. One problem with BrowZine is its emphasis on digital content. When information seekers want to know what journal content a library has, and all the links on the library's webpage direct one to BrowZine, they assume the content reflects the library's complete holdings. Information seekers must know, or be told, to also search the integrated library system (ILS) for the full picture of the library's journal holdings.

ORGANIZATIONAL CULTURE

Trauma affects the ability of victims to seek information, recommendations, and referrals. Adopting trauma-informed principles like trustworthiness and transparency is the next step in creating, rebuilding, or restoring our connectedness to others, whether they are internal or external others. While our ultimate goal is trustworthy and transparent customer service in our libraries, library workers cannot give what they haven't received. This saying appears frequently in self-help and personal growth literature. It has multiple meanings. Many times it refers to self-care. When our emotional bandwidth is tapped out, we are at our least effective when it comes to providing anything above average customer service. Hence, the call for attention to self-care that pervades our lives. Secondly, the saying refers to our own emotional capacity. If we've never known kindness, how can we give it to another? If we've never had a good friend, how can we be one to someone else? Likewise, if we've only worked in libraries where betrayal, information-hoarding, and purposeful miscommunication predominate in the culture, how do we know what the opposite looks and feels like? And better yet, how can we model it? If the library administration is opaque and not trustworthy, how can library workers at service desks embody trustworthiness and transparency for traumatized patrons? They cannot.

Top-down cultural change is required for libraries that want to be trauma-responsive. But this is a two-way street. The library administration must trust their staff to do their best and perform their best while serving patrons. Working in a surveillance state sends the implicit message that workers are not trusted to complete their work with agency and autonomy. Ideally, library administrators hire good people and let them work without any interference or micromanaging. While this may be the official line, or the director's vision, it doesn't always pan out in reality, especially when the director or a manager wants to stage-manage everything, or haggle over details in a workflow whose oversight they have already assigned to someone else, or undermine someone's work by reassigning it to a third party.

A recently retired colleague explained his frustrations about our academic library by comparing it to his twenty years of experience in the military. He said that in the military they assign you a job and expect you to do it, and in the end, you are accountable for the outcomes. But in the library, he said he was given a job and then micromanaged and told how to do it to his supervisor's particular satisfaction. His work was double, even triple checked. This was not on account of any inability on his part to do his job, but rather, it directly reflected his supervisor's unwarranted lack of trust in his skills and experience, and his ability to complete the tasks assigned to him. His supervisor's unwillingness to trust him resulted in frustration for both him and for her. Ultimately, the supervisor's lack of trust stemmed from her need to feel safe, which can often be traced back to overwhelming experiences of childhood trauma and insecurity.

There is practical and emotional trust at all echelons in library operations and services. Practical trust develops when everyone meets their commitments: when everyone shows up on time, everyone contributes their part, and everyone does what they promise they will do. They meet expectations. As part of a team, when one person shirks their duty or cancels their shift at the circulation or reference desk regularly, they are not trusted by their colleagues. They earn a reputation for being incompetent and unreliable. They cannot perform the work or pitch in with the team's efforts to meet the service goals of the library. The resulting lack of communication, duplication of effort, missed deadlines, and poor productivity can erode trust and morale. Emotional trust ties in with library staff meeting their commitments and being held accountable when they fail to meet expectations. Emotional trust depends on all levels in the library clearly communicating about rules, procedures, activities, schedules, and so on. When it comes to working with a team, knowing that your immediate team members have your back contributes to emotional trust. They help out when there are service gaps to fill because staff are out sick, on annual leave, or for some other reason. They support and defend colleagues when someone bears the blame for a poor decision, an incorrect reference answer, or a mistake in the cash register.

A strong commitment from the administration and stakeholders is required for this customer service model to work. All relationships up and down the chain of command must model trust and transparency. Secrecy and secret communications destroy transparency and trust between people and within organizations. After my stepfather returned from treatment for alcoholism and drug addiction, our family's mantra was "Secrets keep us sick," which paraphrases an Alcoholics Anonymous saying, "You're only as sick as your secrets." Library workers whose families have healed from dysfunctions due to addiction can easily recognize a dysfunctional organization by the number of secrets it keeps and the systems (e.g., policies, procedures) it has erected to distort or obfuscate the truth. We can assume that nobody grew up in perfectly functional families, but those who grew up in households with addiction, which is one of the ACE measures of childhood trauma, can help library administrators recognize the unspoken, or even blatant, organizational barriers that limit trust and transparency.

When city commissions or university administrations make sweeping decisions about library buildings or operations without input and assent from the library director, this generates a lack of trust in those stakeholders. Twice in the past ten years, our university administration has mandated sweeping changes to my library that required major space shifts. First, in 2010 we were told to empty the first-floor book stacks, which held about 125,000 volumes, in order to make room for a testing and writing center and an Einstein's Bagel shop. There was no communication with the interim dean, aside from saying that this plan had been decided, so make it happen.

Then, in 2018, without permission or input from the dean of libraries, the first floor was transformed from an information commons into a student area for eating, hanging out, and charging mobile devices because the student center adjacent to the library was closed for a two-year renovation. These sweeping changes erode and destroy trust in our stakeholders.

HONESTY AND DISCRETION

Maintaining trust within networks is a priority in a trauma-informed and trauma-responsive library. In K–12 and academic libraries, for example, the Family Educational Rights and Privacy Act protects students' information. School and academic librarians don't share student information or talk offline about students' grades, scores, or other personal information.

In a trusting and transparent library, confidentiality is honored. For example, when staff take (unpaid) leave under the Family and Medical Leave Act, their reasons are private and should not be gossiped about without their permission. Gradually, though, the reason for their absence circulates within the organization. Gossip is a normal, natural activity for many people. Over time, as we grow more comfortable with our colleagues and share personal information with them, trust builds. It's easy for confidential information to slip from one person's mouth to another's ears in the course of everyday collegial relationships. People providing administrative support know more information about each employee than anyone else. When academic librarians are going through the tenure and promotion process, committee deliberations and decisions should remain confidential until announcements are made by the university president about who earned tenure and who was promoted at the institution. At my academic library, internal knowledge of the results was privately shared with the candidate as a courtesy, unless it was negative, in which case the news arrived as a total surprise upon notification that their bid had been unsuccessful at some level.

While we want to trust our colleagues, not all are trustworthy. We want our patrons to trust us and feel safe. Certainly, it takes time, and negative or positive experience, to learn who to trust in the organization with our information and who we can never trust. As professionals who provide customer service to trauma survivors, conducting ourselves with integrity is elemental and ties in with the earlier section on moral safety.

A colleague of mine who is on the staff was promised a raise for taking on additional duties. When she followed up with the dean and the division head, she was told that Human Resources had declined the raise. But after following up with Human Resources, she learned that nobody from the library had ever contacted them about increasing her salary. What she learned from this experience is that our library administration lacked integrity and could not be trusted.

Many years ago I was offered a different position in my library by our interim dean. I asked to give her my decision when I returned from annual leave in a weeks' time. She agreed to this. When I came back to work, she informed me that another librarian had agreed to take the position while I was away. But there had been no need to rush the decision and place a body in that position immediately. From this point on, I couldn't trust the interim dean because she had betrayed our agreement, and there were no subsequent opportunities to rebuild the lost trust between us.

START WITH A BASELINE

Measuring the baseline level of trust in a library is an important first step in the process of making improvements. Understanding how trust works, and when it doesn't work, can help pinpoint a library's strengths and weaknesses. The questions a library administration can ask to gauge the level of trust include:
- How much do library staff trust the director/dean?
- How can the power differentials between the administration and front-line employees be reduced?
- Is collaboration truly evident or is it faked?
- What kind of silos exist within the library?
- How does information flow between units?
- How is accountability modeled by the leadership?

Once these questions are answered, problems can be addressed, and changes made that develop and potentially sustain a culture of trust. Understanding the work cycle in the library can also help in assessing organizational behavior:
- At what times of the year are the staffers stressed?

- At what times are they disengaged?
- How does this relate to outside influences? For example, for public libraries, how does K–12 being in session affect the daily workflow?
- Likewise, for academic libraries, how do semester-by-semester demands for research consultation and library instruction affect the staff's morale, energy, and their availability for work on other projects?

Pinpointing one area for change at a time allows the library administration to assess whether the change was effective. For example, changing policies about vacation time, travel allowances, or professional development opportunities is an area where allowing staff more autonomy and flexibility may pay off by building trust within the organization. Being transparent about any change is advisable, so that library staff know the reason behind the change, the date it will occur, and how long the policy change will be effective. However, unless the organizational climate is measured prior to the changes, there is no way to chart whether those changes had the desired effect, or an unexpected one. It's possible, and even probable that an optimum level of trust and transparency may never be reached within a library. But continuous improvement toward the ideal is an executable goal. The closer a library is to right, the farther it moves away from wrong. Great customer service cannot occur without trust, nor can trauma-responsive services.

INTERACTING WITH PATRONS

In a trauma-informed library, patrons have adequate time and the library respects them by letting them ask questions and by responding with appropriate answers and information. Allowing space for trauma survivors to be vulnerable, if appropriate, is a cardinal step in trust-building. Typically, there is time and opportunity within the reference interview or research consultation for the librarian and patron to build a rapport and establish a modicum of trust. Listening closely to what the patron says—and what they fail to reveal—can help us gauge the tenor of the interaction. Asking open-ended questions helps our patrons to discover resources and make connections they might never have made on their own. But we should not forcefully push them in the direction that we think they should take. In fact, as we interviewed candidates for reference librarian positions during a recent vacancy, the search committee and I were horrified when one candidate admitted that they strongly pushed people in the "right direction," toward the "right answer," according to their judgment.

As stated earlier, trauma survivors are hypervigilant when it comes to scanning the environment for threats. They easily pick up on disingenuous body language and microexpressions that telegraph deceit or concealed emotions. The body transmits information about our intentions, thoughts, and emotions through our facial expression, posture, and other physical markers. But our words and our body language may not match. Trauma survivors pick up on this discrepancy immediately. While microexpressions can be useful to read someone's intentions, they do not always indicate deception, but may simply suggest uneasiness.

Generally speaking, liars outside of their comfort zone blink rapidly and make irregular or broken eye contact. However, these behaviors may also occur in people who are merely uncomfortable in the library or who are neurodivergent. While it may be that library staff are made uneasy by a patron's information inquiry, working through that discomposure calmly and engaging with the patron can alleviate distrust. Folded arms, legs, or props placed between a patron and librarian present physical barriers that communicate wariness. Hedemark and Lindberg (2018) posit that librarians' bodies are sites of information and communication, and that librarians learn a bodily sense of communicating with patrons through the performance of physical and emotional movements. Their work is based in a perspective where literacy acquisition is viewed as based in corporeal experience, which has interesting implications for libraries working with trauma survivors. Hedemark and Lindberg cite Foucault in regarding bodies acting as texts that can be "read" alongside other cultural expressions. They also cite Annemaree Lloyd (2009), who says essentially the same thing: that librarian's bodies disseminate information through the ways patrons read our bodies.

Thus, library staff should clear the physical space between themselves and the patron as a trust-building practice. Putting one's hands toward or over one's mouth indicates uncertainty about the words coming out. Library staff should train themselves to keep their hands away from their mouths and necks, but also be mindful to keep them clearly visible. Hands hidden in pockets, under tables, or behind one's back feel unsafe to trauma survivors because they cannot see what may be hidden in them, for example, weapons.

Many library workers enjoy ongoing, long-term relationships with patrons. When I was the director of a one-person public library serving a very small community (approximately 5,300 people), I delighted in the relationships I built with retired and middle-aged people, as well as children, who were regular library patrons. Trust developed from my being friendly, open, and showing genuine interest in who they were and how the library could improve their lives. Trust and rewarding relationships built up incrementally over months from a series of positive experiences and relational interactions. In some libraries this is possible, and even probable, but in others, creating and maintaining relationships with patrons that go beyond their brief stop at the circulation or reference desk is difficult, because in school and academic libraries our focus is on teaching patrons information self-sufficiency. We teach them not to need us.

ORGANIZING KNOWLEDGE

Paradoxically, while public libraries are actively building trust, on some level libraries have created distrust regarding the frameworks of knowledge that they collect, store, and preserve. The branch of philosophy called epistemology deals with our beliefs and assumptions about the nature of knowledge; what is and what is not acceptable. Melodie J. Fox (2014) explained epistemology's relevance to library and information science education through its concern with the nature of knowledge, truth, authority, agency, category-formation, and the representation and reliability of all knowledge. While epistemology relates to all aspects of librarianship, it has particular application in school and academic libraries because it informs the pedagogical methods that are used to teach students about information literacy in the classroom. Epistemology also underlies what is and what is not collectable by libraries. Most professions lack the self-reflection necessary to examine their assumptions and biases about information and the nature of knowledge. These unexamined assumptions greatly affect research agendas, theories, methodology, data analysis, conclusions, what is published, and what work within disciplines is collected and promoted by libraries.

Having both internal and external self-identified trauma survivors share their experiences and opinions about the library is essential in the framework of trauma-informed care and is part of the trust-building process. Trauma survivors need to be part of all the processes, from planning to collection-building to weeding, that make up the information life cycle in the library. Many types of libraries have this level of community involvement while some are more standoffish, but this could be because of the way that special libraries operate for their special audiences.

Having said all this, what role do libraries have in the growth, dissemination, and circulation of knowledge? As long-established institutions, libraries have marginalized Indigenous peoples' ways of knowing through their collection policies, cataloging, and classification schemes. Recognizing that our approaches to the organization, cataloging, and classification of the knowledge of Indigenous peoples has aligned with the settler-colonizers can help libraries move toward a trauma-informed approach to operations and customer service. For example, Daniel Day, a fashion designer and haberdasher from Harlem in New York City, talks about how careless record-keeping affected his family. Day is one of seven children born to his parents in the 1940s. In his memoir, *Dapper Dan: Made in Harlem* (2019), he talked about how his siblings' birth names and genders were incorrectly recorded due to systematic racism in the city's vital records office. Similarly, museums, archives, libraries, and other information organizations charged with record-keeping, documentation, and the storage of cultural artifacts have failed and betrayed Indigenous peoples through their lack of accountability. Whether by getting details wrong, or refusing to keep records, or covering up poor record-keeping after the fact, some institutions have created severe barriers to accessing the remaining records of Indigenous people of the past. Australian and Canadian archivists are interrogating these past practices and are working toward reconciliation in a post-colonial landscape.

Acknowledging the epistemological distinctiveness of all communities imparts authenticity to libraries' collections, discovery and metadata, and operations. Once the problem of the systematic settler-colonial marginalization of Indigenous knowledge has been acknowledged, libraries have the opportunity to restore the balance and collaborate with Indigenous communities to more truthfully and correctly restore, describe, and present that information in their collections. Or libraries may even go beyond these measures to repatriation and return primary documents to the safekeeping of the Indigenous communities where they originated. Moving beyond the established documentary canon of any discipline to discover and include noncanonical information is imperative for knowledge creation and management. Our written and published documents can't keep up with the pace of change and the discovery of new problems and new ways of solving them.

But why the emphasis on epistemology? Why should librarians concern themselves with knowledge production, when libraries are viewed as mere storehouses of information; librarians merely collect the resources and then refer users to them. Our collections are sometimes criticized for their relevance and their meaningfulness. And it is true that our epistemological and ethical assumptions about knowledge and how we arrive at truths shape our practice as librarians. For example, if we collect religious works, there is a canon that includes an enormous body of religious scriptures, interpretation, commentary, analysis, and so on. However, if a library is affiliated with or funded by a particular religious body or sect, its collection's holdings may well be skewed in favor of the worldview of the funding institution. In many cases, collection policies that specifically encourage the acquisition of materials that support the funding institution's religious tenets are expected and standard. College and university libraries attached to the Nazarene, Baptist, Methodist, Jewish, and Mormon denominations, to name a few, most likely legitimize the preponderance of materials supporting those specific worldviews in their collections as a strength, a special collection.

What library staff *does* matters. And how we do it matters, as well. Our professional expertise and knowledge are put to good use when we respond with factual evidence and data to counter "fake news" and "alternative facts." Since 2016 the public's trust in both the government and the media has eroded. Gallup reported that Americans' trust in the media recently plummeted to an all-time low of 32 percent. And by April 2019, according to the Pew Research Center, only 17 percent of Americans said they trust the U.S. government. This steep decline demonstrates a widespread belief that either the media or the government (or both) are rife with disinformation and fake news. Librarians' informational skills and expertise can provide critical help to our communities in developing the information literacy they need when faced with politicians who twist the facts and manipulate the public trust with their "fake news" rhetoric. Most Americans don't feel any interest in analyzing the media's biases, but they should. Librarians are the stopgap here and must step in with guidance about how to evaluate media content. In school and academic libraries, we can establish class projects around fact-checking and show students why verifying the statements made in the media (and by our political leaders) is in their own best interest. Accordingly, identifying data sources and critically examining their credibility and purpose enables our patrons to better understand who is attempting to influence them, and why. A free press is critical to a democratic and open society.

THE PUBLIC TRUST

Libraries rely upon their well-established reputation in the community as authoritative and credible sources of information. Libraries are trusted institutions because of their values, their beliefs, and their commitment to individual privacy and freedom of information. But how have we failed, or failed to reach, the groups that don't use us? Likewise, how do we change our reputation with people who don't trust us? Are they also the ones who avoid both our buildings and online resources? How do we demonstrate our trustworthiness to non-users, especially when they've been burned, or found our services or resources irrelevant and unhelpful?

Pew Research data established librarians as among the most trusted professionals in the United States. We're parallel with health care providers and well above social media influencers, government agencies, and news and media outlets. Perhaps patrons and community members aren't familiar with librarians' professional ethics like the Library Code of Ethics. Our commitment to those ethics shines through our practices, and conceivably that accounts for a portion of the public's trust in our work and our spaces. Furthermore, libraries are local entities. Library staff are known and are easily accountable to the community they serve. We are invested in our communities and serve many of their information needs. We're also motivated by a shared purpose of bettering our communities and helping students of all ages succeed in school. These professional qualities and characteristics align with Ettarh's thoughts on vocational awe. Ettarh believes that librarians are good, noble, and self-sacrificing in the gendered way that all feminized professions are—nurses, teachers, social workers, and so on. We are approachable, we are someone's neighbor, and we are relevant. Listening carefully is one of our strengths, but how can we leverage that and take it to a trauma-responsive level? Or is this one of the areas where we've unwittingly been meeting the precepts all along?

Andreas Varheim (2014) talks about the reasons why public libraries are producers of trust and social capital. He says it's because they offer access to universal information and space to everyone. Libraries also strive to treat everyone equally. Varheim's qualitative interviews suggest that public libraries create social trust. His 2014 study indicated that library programming increased social trust within a targeted population of Mexican immigrants. This population distrusts government institutions but was convinced to participate in public library programming based upon advocacy and word of mouth from their friends who demonstrated that public libraries can be trusted.

Trust can also erode. Jill Lepore (2018), an American history professor at Harvard University, argues that universities are complicit in letting sources of government funding set their intellectual agendas. Academic libraries either grow or contract their collections and services in response to government agendas or partisanship. As a result, both immigrants and longtime citizens may come to view public and academic libraries with distrust.

As noted earlier, one strategy for bolstering the public's trust, and specifically our patrons' trust in our libraries, is to be transparent about library procedures. These procedures should be clearly written, and they should be predictable. There should not be special treatment or barriers waived for certain individuals. For example, at my university, swiping an ID card for entry into the gymnasium is required by everyone. However, I've noticed that when the university's president and his entourage enter the building for meetings held in the space, they are waved through and the procedure for swiping ID cards is bypassed. Certainly, this demonstrates that some of us are privileged, while some of us are not. Likewise, my university is a dry campus. Nobody is allowed to have wine or beer at university-sponsored events. The president's on-campus gatherings, however, are exceptions to this rule.

Building trust and loyalty starts with listening to the voices and concerns of everyone and including them in the process, whatever that may be, and at whatever level they feel comfortable with. Public libraries, for example, can establish teen advisory groups who help create an authentic experience for that demographic. Listening to teens at this level turns them into valued stakeholders. Improving the library based upon their reactions can help the library provide trauma-informed customer service. Teens can often steer collection-building in areas like anime, manga, graphic novels, and young adult literature. They volunteer at events, and they can advise on what types of programming and events the library should have to attract and engage more teens. They can even consult with librarians and directors about what changes to spaces and policies will attract teens and keep them in the library. Many teens need these kinds of activities to fulfill community service hours for higher education scholarships, and so two equally important purposes are served.

7

Peer Support

Peer support is when people provide the benefit of their knowledge and experience, or provide some other kind of help, to each other. Peer support is distinguished from other kinds of support by the fact that it is provided by a "peer," an equal, such as a coworker or colleague in a library. Peer support (and mutual self-help) are strategies that trauma-informed practitioners can use to help establish safe spaces and professional practices, build and rebuild trust, value and encourage collaboration, and serve as models of trauma-informed and trauma-responsive librarians. The peer support that we offer to our fellow librarians or that we receive from our patrons is based on shared values and principles. This support is voluntary. The key elements in providing peer support are to be nonjudgmental, empathetic, respectful, and reciprocal.

PEER SUPPORT IN YOUTH SERVICES

Teens can play a vital role in peer support. First, you should identify how the library offers any access to peer support for the teens using its services. Next, examine what barriers exist to implementing peer support within the library.

Models for the peer support of library patrons exist in some form in some libraries. If they do not exist, then thinking about opportunities for growth is important in fulfilling this component of trauma-informed customer services. Many public libraries have teen advisories and teen volunteers. Teen advisors can consult with librarians and directors about programming, spaces, collections, and possibly at some level of customer service. Teen volunteers may serve roles in programming and may also help with shelving recently circulated books and periodicals.

Another possibility is training teen volunteers to staff a teen-specific information desk in the teen or children's area wherein they answer directional, reader's advisory, and simple reference questions. Understanding teens' limits is an essential component of their training, however, and they should feel encouraged to refer difficult questions to professionals. Naturally, there are some problems with this proposal. First, being dependent on volunteers to staff service desks can be problematic, as is finding a number of committed, reliable teens to staff a teen information desk. But it is a provocative idea, one that larger public libraries with vibrant teen engagement might pilot, with teen volunteers pairing with librarians who mentor and coach them. Such a pilot would at least answer some questions: How effective is this model? How supported do the teens feel by their peers? How approachable are the teens? How well do the teens perform as peer support? How can we adapt this for scale?

Alternatively, we can follow the pop-up model used by the Chattanooga (TN) Public Library. Their pop-up model responds to clusters of teen bodies in the building. When librarians see a group of teens or tweens, they turn on a movie, play with LEGOs, or pull out a robot and invite patron participation. Interestingly, their assessments prove, at least in their community, that being actively mobile and interacting with teen patrons is key for the success of this model.

Another idea is to collaborate with the public school system or other agencies to develop after-school peer-tutoring for and by teens. Similarly, establishing peer-tutoring or peer reference in the K–12 library meets the goal of peer support for trauma-informed libraries. Both of these models, again, depend on the labor of volunteers. But many teens are required, for a variety of reasons, to serve their community in a nonprofit organization or other entity for a certain number of hours each month or quarter. Working together with teens in this fashion serves both their needs and those of the public library. A striking example of this use of teens for peer support is Varheim's aforementioned work with Mexican immigrants participating in ESL classes in public libraries; he found that cultivating these Mexican youth and having them advocate for the public library and act as ambassadors to their community of undocumented immigrants was the best way to build trust in the public library among them.

Alternatively, having students who are serving detention or spending days in in-school suspension offer peer support in K–12 libraries may give them the opportunity they need to work with a trauma-informed and trauma-responsive staff. The documentary *Paper Tigers* (2015) should be essential viewing for K–12 school librarians. This documentary follows six teens at Lincoln Alternative High School in Walla Walla (WA) as the school transitions from a traditional approach to a trauma-informed school. Witnessing the transformation and successes (and some failures) of at-risk teens when they're treated with trauma-responsiveness is enlightening. The documentary, and the literature, both agree that the most effective intervention in traumatized children's and teen's lives is having one adult who mentors, coaches, and unconditionally loves and cares for them. The adult doesn't have to be a family member, or even interact with them daily.

Liz Murray is the cofounder of the Arthur Project (a Bronx-based mentoring project for at-risk middle school students), the author of *Breaking Night: A Memoir of Forgiveness, Survival, and My Journey from Homeless to Harvard* (2010), and the subject of the TV film *Homeless to Harvard: The Liz Murray Story* (2003). She attributes her success to two mentors she had while growing up as the child of two addicts in the Bronx in New York City. Her first mentor was an upstairs neighbor, Arthur, and her second was a teacher at the high school where she graduated at the top of her class after attending for two years.

School and public librarians can be those mentoring adults. We already are. Consider the numbers of writers, poets, playwrights, and other creative people who attribute their success to a love of reading, and time spent at the library as a child. Among them are Barbara Kingsolver, Neil Gaiman, Nikki Giovanni, Amy Tan, Kiese Laymon, Annie Proulx, and Julia Alvarez. Some of our most creative people have found respite in our libraries, and the safety and care they found there contributed to their later achievements.

PEER SUPPORT IN ACADEMIC LIBRARIES

Academic librarians bemoan the greying of the profession, and how having younger librarians or graduate students staff our service desks may make our libraries more engaging and approachable by the undergraduate student population. Many of our students, and patrons of all types of libraries, experience anxiety related to our spaces or services. Some students may fear librarians because of negative past experiences they've had when interacting with us, or they may even be influenced by the detrimental stereotypes of librarians promoted by our culture and media. Morris, Conteh, and Harris-Perry describe a case in *Pushout: The Criminalization of Black Girls in Schools* (2016) wherein a black trauma survivor's major trigger was "older white women" because of very negative past experiences she'd had with them. According to data from 2009, 83 percent of librarians are women, and 89 percent of all librarians, male and female, are white. Moreover, 64 percent of librarians are 45 years or older, while 40 percent are over age 55. So characterizing librarians as "older white women" is appropriate here. Keer and Carlos suggest that librarians can remediate the "older white women" stereotype by advocating for marginalized groups within the library and in their communities.

In a similar vein, as our profession develops core cultural competence skills, the stereotype of the "older white woman" may diminish. Those core skills align with a trauma-informed approach: being open and nonjudgmental, valuing diversity, self-care, willingness to learn, social justice, and caring. Older white women can mitigate librarian stereotypes by advocating for trauma-informed change within their organization.

Adult students may feel awkward, overwhelmed, confused, or inadequate when entering academic libraries. Librarians acknowledge this anxiety. Academic librarians studied this problem, and developed interventions for anxiety reduction in our spaces that specifically targeted apprehensive students. When students assume that visiting the library is a negative experience, we should look closely to examine whether some of this anxiety occurs because of our current policies, procedures, and practices, or whether it is a perception based on past events, which may be reasonably correlated with historical industry-wide practices.

Liz Murray explained that a universal and long-term effect of childhood traumatization is a pervasive feeling of not belonging. She says that there is a wall between trauma survivors and the rest of "straight" society. The "otherness" of trauma separates these children and adults from feelings of belonging and acceptance. It prevents them from speaking up in class, speaking up at work, or speaking up at all. The omnipresent feeling of being "other" and separate can inflict long-term damage on a person's psyche. Overcoming this sense of not belonging can take a lifetime of work.

A number of university and college librarians have established peer reference and peer instruction programs in their libraries. And for good reason, since research in academia reveals that classroom and residential peers have a significant influence on the intellectual development and learning behaviors of the student body. Certainly, these programs offer mutual opportunities for student and organizational growth and effectiveness. But while there are dozens of examples of viable service models for peer reference, the evidence for the effectiveness of undergraduates giving library instruction to their peers is only modest.

One item that has not been incorporated in this innovative service model is the trauma-informed approach. Yes, undergraduate peer-reference providers are taught the steps of the reference interview and are taught how to be approachable, demonstrate inclusion, maintain confidentiality, and remain neutral about information. They learn how to navigate print and electronic resources, but most importantly, trauma survivors understand where their skills end and when to refer their peers to a librarian.

PEER SUPPORT IN LIBRARY ORGANIZATIONS

The best place to begin here is with the question: Do we offer peer support for our staff? Why or why not? And if not, where do we start? What is it about the model of peer support that benefits our operations and customer service models? There are multiple opportunities for building peer support within libraries. You can start with the onboarding process. For longtime employees, you can provide professional development opportunities. And you can create an organizational culture of support. You should try to set up everyone for success. Success looks different across different organizations, but it should have the same goal of facilitating the connection and support between coworkers. If you're unsure of what peer support looks like or how it works, one example that many people are aware of is Weight Watchers. Weight Watchers is a peer support group for people who wish to lose, maintain, or gain weight within a formalized program that offers them support. Likewise, Alcoholics Anonymous, Narcotics Anonymous, Overeaters Anonymous, and Al-Anon serve particular peer support networks and bring together people with different levels of experience with the subject. Generally, peer support groups stimulate a culture of wellness in organizations, communities, and ultimately, in individuals.

Some libraries offer employee assistance programs (EAPs), which provide counseling, assessments, and referrals to employees who are having personal or work-related problems that can affect their job performance. Libraries offer EAPs to their employees via their umbrella organization, such as the state for K–12 school libraries, the city/state/county for public libraries, and the state for public colleges and universities. The services provided by EAPs are effective and can be of great benefit to library workers struggling with interpersonal relationships, financial stresses, legal issues, emotional problems, and substance use issues, but developing and maintaining internal and informal peer support should be a library's primary goal.

Creating peer support systems within organizations enhances positive behaviors and can transform cold, indifferent cultures into ones that are trauma-informed, warm, and emotionally open. Peer support builds on the networks that friends and colleagues instinctively offer each other in healthy organizational cultures. Look at what your library is already doing that fits within the trauma-informed model. Some elements present within peer support include mentoring, peer professional development, mediation and conflict resolution, listening, buddying, and advocacy. Your library probably already engages in some of these activities and initiatives.

Of course, as with any new idea proposed in libraries, there are steps to take before implementing a peer support system. First, you need to generate awareness of the need for peer support and its potential positive effects on library workers and the organizational culture, so educating everyone about this is a beginning. Once awareness has been engendered, doing a needs analysis for the group of library workers you want to serve is the next step in the process. Peer support systems often fail because those in charge decide on one approach, apply it, and then it turns out to be ineffective. They don't learn from this failure; instead of trying again with a different approach, they just write off the whole endeavor as a lost cause. You should survey the lay of the land, so to speak, by conducting a needs assessment of library workers in a unit or in the whole library in order to identify the needs of the workers, and then you should assess what resources are already in place to meet those needs. Performing a needs assessment may reveal that some peer support structures are already in place, but careful examination may also reveal barriers to peer support that need to be removed. The data gathered from a small, anonymous, five- to ten-item questionnaire asking library workers about their perceptions of peer support can identify any gaps and barriers. The questions should be constructed along the following lines, and the answers should occupy a Likert scale for easy analysis:

1. If I wanted to talk to a coworker about work issues, there are several whom I trust.
2. If I was sick, I could easily find a coworker to cover my shift/work.
3. When I need help figuring out a problem at work, I can easily find someone whom I trust to speak with.
4. I can easily find someone to sit with and talk to at social events sponsored by my library.
5. There are coworkers and managers who can provide the support I need to excel in my job.

Conducting a small-scale survey of this type allows the library administration to measure the scope of the problems and discuss the various routes for intervention. There are various measures like the Social Relations Index, the Workplace Health Survey, Social Support Scale, and Support Climate that can be used by libraries for this purpose. The results should provide enough guidance so that those steering the committee for peer support can determine where the problems lie. Are there library workers who feel lonely and excluded? Are there feelings of distrust? Are levels of collegiality measurable? To what extent is bullying an issue? How accessible are managers and supervisors? Does the organizational climate indicate a cultural problem?

Analyzing the results of the survey leads to figuring out one or multiple interventions or can help the library administration to prioritize where the most urgent needs lie. Deciding at which level to intervene takes much thought, and implementing those interventions, likewise, takes much planning and coordination. A systematic intervention will look at the intrapersonal, interpersonal, organizational, community, and policy levels. The intrapersonal level focuses on the library administration creating and circulating documentation,

educational, and marketing materials that espouse the trauma-informed attitudes and beliefs the library has adopted. The interpersonal level denotes the
buddy system, or the peer support system that is active and operational within
the library. Organizational-level interventions include evaluations in which
library workers document their awareness of trauma-informed practice, such
as reviewing an interaction with a patron and making notes about how the
worker used empathy or collaboration within the exchange. Community-level
interventions instituted by libraries include the public recognition of library
workers who champion trauma-informed approaches in their work. And
finally, policy-level interventions may include merit pay for library workers
who demonstrate effectiveness and sustained trauma-informed approaches to
customer service.

PEER SUPPORTERS

Those who provide peer support in libraries should be trauma-informed
"champions." Ideally, they are either well-versed in TIC's principles and practices, wholeheartedly committed to this cultural change, or are themselves
trauma survivors. And they should be "peers," that is, the hierarchical equals
of those whom they are helping. For very hierarchical libraries, there should
be at least one person serving as peer support in each tier or level of the hierarchy. The point of peer support is to link up a worker with a coworker who
has a shared experience and who can offer a range of support, or perhaps
refer that worker to an outside agency which can address serious issues. One
example of peer support in organizations is programs established to improve
workers' physical health based upon a public health model of intervention,
which focuses on prevention. These programs are established to help with
chronic disease management and to reach marginalized or hard-to-engage
workers who lack access to care and support. In very large organizations that
promote health interventions, there may be separate peer support groups
that target and sustain workers with diabetes, heart disease, cancer, obesity,
and so on.

　　Research into bullying in the workplace suggests that creating peer support systems may be an effective antidote to this problem. Likewise, research
into gendered workplace incivility suggests that administrative fostering of
social support networks, either formal or informal, is a means of engaging
library workers who feel marginalized, isolated, and excluded by the broader
library culture. Another aspect of this process includes giving ownership of the
system to library workers and developing roles that the participants can play.
The ideal person to provide peer support in the library is a good listener, is
empathetic, has good problem-solving skills, and is willing to serve in this role
for their colleagues. A good listener is an active listener who mirrors what the
person is saying with a response like "It seems like you're having a problem."

The listener restates what she thinks the coworker is saying so that they can calibrate and have a mutual understanding of the problem at hand. Misinterpreting what people say is very easy, especially for those of us who are saddled with personal and professional baggage. We often interpret the experiences of others through our own perspectives. Those perspectives can be skewed or informed by either very bad or very good experiences in the library. Being a Pollyanna is just as unhelpful as being a Negative Nancy. Understanding this and maintaining a level of objectivity is the best approach to take.

MENTOR PROGRAMS

Mentoring and/or coaching is one example of something that libraries already do, both formally and informally. The difference between mentoring and coaching is slight, but tangible. According to Forbes.com, *mentors* are successful in their knowledge domain and share their hard-won expertise in their field as a response to the problems the mentee brings them. On the other hand, *coaches* anticipate problems and address specific challenges, like helping transition a coworker to a trauma-informed approach. A mentoring/coaching process is seen as a win-win situation for both the established librarian and the newbie. Newbies receive socialization into the profession and the library's culture, while mentors can actively change negative aspects of their library's organizational culture by emphatically communicating and guiding the newbie in the positive behaviors the library seeks to embody.

As far as mentoring/coaching goes in libraries, it's all good. Mentoring helps new library workers develop a sense of belonging. The support the senior person provides is also effective for retention. Additionally, mentoring within a context of cultural change, such as shifting to a trauma-informed culture, has great potential for enhancing those library workers who have been historically excluded or marginalized by libraries.

INDIVIDUAL ACTIONS

On a more informal level, each of us can take tiny actions that contribute to peer support and a trauma-informed approach without going through the long, top-down process of instituting a formal peer support system in a library. When the library leadership resists cultural change, either because they doubt its effectiveness or they believe it's too much work, sometimes the only thing we can change is how we personally think about things and how we conduct ourselves as professionals. Moreover, external avenues for peer support exist outside our libraries in our local communities, as well as online. E-mail distribution lists can provide help with technical problems, though not so much the kind of peer support that we desperately need and lack from our organizations. The Facebook group Library Think Tank- #ALATT offers a great deal of peer support and feedback on technical issues, as well as on more interpersonal ones. Jules Shore, a librarian at the National Library of Medicine, mediates an anonymous question-and-answer function on the page, where those who are grappling with major professional issues, or need peer support and advice from those with a similar experience, can find answers and potentially connect one-on-one with advice-givers.

One informal action we can take in our libraries is to find ourselves a female friend, or "work wife," in our workplace. As a concept, this creates the peer support that librarians need while countering the expectation in the library workplace that women are invariably pitted against other women. Erica Cerulo and Claire Mazur, the authors of *Work Wife: The Power of Female Friendship to Drive Successful Business* (2019), say the practice reconceives the masculine workplace of competition, paving the way for a reimagined organization that values qualities like compassion, mutual support, and transparency.

Cerulo and Mazur recommend bonding with a potential work wife on the basis of shared interests like sanity, yoga, needlework, and so on. Or, if nobody presently fits the bill, developing a mutual passion over something the two of you have in common is a possibility. Senior librarians and managers can play matchmaker by pairing potential wives on the basis of two librarians' personality, family, religion, identity, and so on.

Cerulo and Mazur suggest that fostering a successful work wife partnership leads to collaboration on both a personal and professional level. They identify the characteristics anchoring female friendships as emotional intimacy, vulnerability, instinctual collaboration, and a distinct system of peer support. These dynamics in the professional sphere can have positive effects on library organizations because they create the foundations for peer support, thus aligning with the ultimate goal of trauma-informed customer services.

Another small practice if you are interested in cultivating a culture of care is to check in regularly with team members, direct reports, and others in the library with whom you work. Add five minutes to your daily tasks and visit your colleagues' work areas every day. Take a moment to chat with them and inquire about their day. Pay close attention to their body language, energy level, and their reactions. A small action like this performed daily can develop rapport and peer support among your immediate circle of influence and creates a potential for the practice to spread across all levels in the library. Checking in with those whom you supervise each day develops your professional relationships. It demonstrates care and it offers an ongoing opportunity to help someone in need. Another recommended action within this context is asking how you can help. Can you proofread a document for a coworker? Double-check their LibGuide for broken links? Can you cover their lunch or their break from a public service desk? Or proofread their slides for a presentation? Actively lightening coworkers' burdens by helping with their workflow issues is a form of peer support.

8

Collaboration and Mutuality

Sharing power between library workers and patrons and between library workers and the library administration is what collaboration and mutuality are all about in a trauma-informed approach. This kind of shared decision-making can and does occur between all levels of workers, including library professionals, housekeeping and security personnel, and subcontractors. Shared power optimizes and improves customer service across the organization and its operations, collections, and programs.

Collaboration and mutuality thrive in libraries where the organizational structure is relatively flat. But the more infrastructure and hierarchy an organization builds, and which the workers must navigate, the less simple is the process of collaboration for everyone. Libraries, like other organizations, can have silos within them, or else they can be unified and collaborative, with leadership modeling those values. These levels of integration and compartmentalization occur along a continuum.

Collaboration is working with someone to produce or create something. Everyone collaborates, to some extent, in their personal and professional lives. In a family, planning vacations, choosing where to eat or what to cook, and what to stream after shared meals all require working with others to attain shared goals. And in a library, working with both colleagues and patrons is essential, given the type of work that library staff do. Connecting with others, meeting deadlines, remaining engaged, and working toward innovations are other forms of collaboration.

Library staff collaborate with one another, with patrons, and with community organizations as well. The collaborative team works together by sharing ideas and thinking aloud to accomplish a common goal—in this case, trauma-informed customer service. This type of work requires establishing and maintaining interpersonal relationships, team problem-solving, and keen communication skills.

Lisa Kwan (2019) writes about collaborative initiatives and how leaders tend to focus on logistics, processes, incentives, and outcomes. She says that in doing this, they forget to understand how those being asked to collaborate view the process. They may be expected to give up responsibilities they're comfortable with and skilled at, as well as having to sacrifice the autonomy they're usually allowed in their workflow. Individuals asked to collaborate with others may even find the experience threatening. They can become defensive as a means of guarding their reputations or purviews. These kinds of failed attempts at collaboration can harm all future team efforts. Kwan says that leaders who want more collaboration between teams should assess the resistance and identify where the barriers to true and meaningful collaboration lie. For instance, if there are territorial issues—say, where one group is not in charge and another group's opinion is the only one that matters—then work should be done to address that issue. Likewise, overt inter-group attacks, power plays, covert means of blocking progress, and covert manipulation of boundaries are all symptoms of a culture that is desperately in need of work to neutralize negative team dynamics.

It's obvious to everyone that having a shared vision or goal is the first step in cultivating collaboration. For example, shifting to a trauma-informed approach to library services requires convincing library staff that this change in thinking can and should affect all parts of the library. Being trauma-informed is compelling enough in itself to inspire library staff to accomplish the transformation. There is clear evidence that shifting to a trauma-informed organization has multiple benefits for library workers, library patrons, and the community at large. But when goals and objectives are presented to a library organization haphazardly, unclearly, or without passion from leadership, library workers will find many reasons to shirk collaboration.

For collaboration at any level to succeed, minimum standards must be communicated. Roles and responsibilities should be clearly delineated. Working at cross-purposes and duplications of effort are frustrating and can be morale killers. When clarity is conveyed by the library administration and leadership, crossing into someone else's purview happens less, and thus fewer conflicts arise. Each person in a collaborative library team takes responsibility for their role and is held accountable for their results. Changing from individual responsibility to team responsibility for processes, procedures, and customer services can form a unified group that collaborates for the library's good.

As libraries foster collaborative functioning in their teams, recognizing and rewarding collaborative behavior reinforces those values that are driving the organization. Professional affirmation is key to helping everyone feel that they are working together for the good of the community they serve. Collaboration requires a high level of trust between those expected to perform within these work dynamics. In a trauma-informed library that has made changes in the areas of trust and transparency, the workers should be able to collaborate effectively to reach their goals and objectives.

MUTUALITY

Mutuality is a way of existing in respectful relation to others and is a necessary component of healthy personal and professional relationships. Studies of mutuality in the health care industry demonstrate that, as a relationship dynamic, it creates close, caring, and effective relationships between providers and clients. Other positives associated with mutuality include better problem resolution, improved accountability, and decreased costs. Mutuality is reciprocal. Another way to consider mutuality is that it lies at the center of a continuum, with the extremes of paternalism and autonomy occurring at each end.

But what does mutuality look like in libraries? If we look at the reference interview, for example, we see the interaction as shared in common. Each person brings strengths and information to the situation as equals in collaboration. They progress toward a common goal—finding an answer, not finding an answer, or referring the patron to another librarian, library, or external resource. Finally, there should be a sense of satisfaction for all involved. The patron's information need is met—or is potentially being met—and they feel confident that the library staff have helped them to the best of their ability. Conversely, the library staff feel satisfied that the question was answered, or they feel frustrated because the patron's inquiry cannot be answered. Like most librarians, they mull over the question and don't give up on finding the answer until it is determined there is none.

When library staff encounter topics they know nothing about, they are responsible for doing the work necessary to ramp up their knowledge of that domain. Likewise, when they discover that their collections are inadequate in a trending area, they are responsible for suggesting or making purchases that address and fill the gap in the collection.

ABOUT LANGUAGE AND NAMING

The language that we use and the words that we select for services, collections, programs, and even for our users set up expectations or dynamics within our relationships. Therefore, if we're committed to working in a trauma-informed framework, mindfulness about naming is essential. This is especially true in the domain of collaboration and mutuality. The Buddhist nun Pema Chodron (2019) quotes the fourteenth-century yogi Longchampa, who says that how we label things is how they appear. Considerate naming should suffuse the library's practices. How we talk about our communities is important because it sets up and sustains the relationship dynamic. Consider the many ways libraries describe the individuals whom we serve: patrons, clients, customers, users, visitors, guests, members, and regulars.

The term *customers* suggests relationships based on transactions where money for goods and services changes hands. By contrast, the term *patrons* suggest "patrons of the arts," those who support opera, orchestras, and art museums. These benefactors give money and gifts, provide endorsement, and spend their time and effort in advocating the organization's mission. In the past two or three decades, libraries of all types have been bombarded with business models as ideal means of managing services. These models emphasize notions of customers getting value for their money, a return on their investment, or efficient service. The models also set up the expectation that the customer is always right, but this can be problematic in college and university libraries, where some students expect librarians to proofread and read their papers, complete literature reviews for them, complete library assignments for them, and so on.

Anecdotally, the idea of "customers" has entered into the realm of local politics, at least in my immediate county. I have served as an election official in my city/county for nearly two decades at the same voting precinct. One of the officers would bring voters over to my station in the polling place, whether I was working as a registrar, voting machine operator, provisional judge, or judge, and introduce them to me as, "I have another customer for you." I didn't correct her, but I should have. They are "citizens" or "voters," not customers.

Likewise, the term *clients* suggests contexts where money for certain services changes hands: therapy, legal services, hairdressing and cosmetology, and so on. The term *users*, while more neutral, is pejorative and is associated with people struggling with addiction. The terms *visitors*, *guests*, *members*, and *regulars* offer more room for neutral dynamics and relationships, although they convey subtle differences in meaning. *Visitors* signifies a short-term relationship, as does *guests*. They both presume a level of hospitality, access to materials, and access to library workers' expertise. *Members* suggests exclusivity, or an exchange of money that endows those persons with a special, elevated, or long-term status and consideration within the library. *Regulars* suggests a carefully constructed relationship built upon repeated contact and mutuality. Conversely, the term *regulars* is also associated with the steady customers in bars. While most of these ways of identifying people in our libraries are problematic, perhaps your library can arrive at a term that carries the least baggage, or you can select an altogether different but appropriate word.

In an earlier chapter, I wrote about the problems with using terms like *problem patrons*, *difficult patrons*, or even *atypical patrons*. When we label groups of people using our libraries in negative ways, these words provide a framework and expectation around the roles that library staff and patrons play in the presumed oppositional dynamic. In fall 2019, I attended a training session readying our graduate assistants for the semester. The supervisor used the term *frequent flyers* to categorize a group of troublesome people who use the library. These "frequent flyers" avoid librarians and graduate assistants and instead look for young female student workers at the Ask Us desk whom they can bully. The term *frequent flyer* is pejorative, not friendly. The supervisor warned the trainees that we have people using the library who behave this way with everyone, not just pretty young women. When the supervisor sees them enter the building, the supervisor walks up to the service desk and protects all the workers, including student ones, from dealing with people who need more care and time than they are trained to handle.

Another area for consideration is how we name our libraries' services or divisions. Though academic libraries are all structured differently, they typically have librarians or departments that are responsible for instruction. These librarians offer "one-shot" instruction for students when professors bring them to the library for learning about databases and online catalogs. Often the library department that provides these services is called "Reference and Instruction" or "Research and Instruction." But using the word *instruction* is tricky, even though that's how we characterize that dynamic between librarian and students. Our concept of the librarian/teacher and student relationship is based on the banking model of education, also called the "empty vessel" model, which assumes that teachers are experts who possess all the knowledge, while students are empty receptacles that the teachers fill with knowledge. This creates a hierarchical power dynamic in which the teacher has more power and authority than the students. This type of hierarchical relationship is what the principles of collaboration and mutuality within trauma-informed approaches set out to dismantle or neutralize. In Paulo Freire's influential book *Pedagogy of the Oppressed* (1968), critical pedagogy is based upon a reciprocal relationship steeped in democracy in which everyone in the relationship symbiotically creates and experiences opportunities for learning. Likewise, feminist pedagogy sets up learning environments as collaborative, democratic spaces in which value is given to a variety of epistemologies as revealed via personal testimony.

Thus, removing the term *instruction* sets up neutral, even potentially positive expectations and assumptions about the learning environment. Changing a department's name from "Research and Instruction" to "Research and

Learning" signifies this fundamental shift in academic librarians' approach to learning environments and the dynamics between individuals engaged in mutual learning. College and university libraries such as the University of Washington, Guilford College, Columbia University, and the University of Pittsburgh use *learning* rather than *instruction* to identify these services and functions.

A reconsideration of how our spaces, departments, and services are named is timely, significant work for libraries. We must use every opportunity to convey our trauma-informed values and beliefs by choosing words wisely. Some may argue that this is part of marketing or branding the library, and if it is, so be it. This is another area in which libraries can claim or reframe their current practices within a trauma-informed structure.

9

Empowerment, Voice, and Choice

The trauma-informed values of empowerment, voice, and choice align closely with many libraries' designs and initiatives undertaken in recent decades to change a stagnant, punitive user experience into an engaging and meaningful one in our real and virtual spaces. From the start, libraries have created service models based upon their historic role as gatekeepers of information, mediators of collections, and arbiters of decorum. Based upon their organization and classification schemes, libraries were set up to reflect the conservative concerns and practices associated with asset management. Over the years we've changed our service and delivery models to empower patrons with as much agency and autonomy over accessing information and resources as possible. This includes involving patrons in website design through all stages; convening focus groups to inquire about their experiences and what changes will serve their needs better; asking patrons to complete surveys; and gathering qualitative data via conversations and anecdote collection. Part of this is fueled by changes across other industries that libraries have adopted in order to remain relevant and create value for patrons. Another reason for our changes is a pragmatic one: dwindling dollars, rising costs, and the inability to maintain adequate staffing levels. Thus, involving patrons in service design kills two birds with one stone. We attempt to provide tailored services and draw upon the energy, time, and labor of our patrons to help us be all things to all people.

EMPOWERMENT

Giving patrons enhanced roles within the organization via shared decision-making and shared goal setting supports trauma-informed practices. Letting trauma survivors help with strategic planning and long-term decision-making, as well as with developing objectives and measuring outcomes, gives libraries greater insight into operational optimization.

Starting with a captive audience can provide quick and easy wins for library administrators and boost their confidence when it comes to effecting change by empowering various patron demographics. In public libraries, the board members and trustees typically support and advocate for the organization within the community. Conducting trauma-informed awareness, education, and training with board members may help the library administration identify and select persons with traumatic childhoods, or high ACEs scores, who can provide insight and represent those interests within the governing body. And, in fact, given board members' role in policy establishment for library operations, their governance position is such that it necessitates their involvement and participation in transforming the library's organizational structure and daily workflow into the trauma-informed model.

In higher education, library deans and directors are typically granted scope and latitude for changing policies and procedures unless they directly involve fines, fees, or financial interests. For these latter types of changes authorization must come from the president's office, or even from the university's state governing body, if it's a public institution. Other types of libraries, whether special or K–12, are ultimately governed by the state department of education.

However, recruiting advisors from the "top" as a strategy may serve to replicate the status quo. Recruiting from the middle and the margins is advisable for a well-balanced group whose interests diverge and align across a continuum. Frankly, the typical suspects serving on library boards or as trustees are well established in the local power structure, and depending on the diversity of the locality, people of color or people marginalized by their identity are rarely integrated into libraries' governing or advisory organizations. But the overly systematic cherry-picking of people of color and marginalized groups can backfire as well. In wanting to ensure diversity, we can pick people solely because of one part of their identity, instead of the wealth of value and insight they may be able to bring to library operations.

Empowering patrons begins by inviting them behind the scenes into the library's processes and governance. Identifying certain patrons as "super-us-ers" is one strategy for reaching out to assemble an advisory board. Following up with patrons who contacted the library administration because they had a complaint or suggestion about solving a problem they encountered with cus-tomer services should be standard practice. Furthermore, these patrons can be invited to participate in advisory activities.

Peer support is essential in helping both patrons and library workers feel empowered. Creating and relying on a supportive network helps increase indi-viduals' feelings of sustained affirmation by peers. Empowering patrons and library workers begins with building on the strengths they already have and mitigating weaknesses by scaffolding upon those areas of strength.

Empowered patrons and library workers will tend to hold libraries accountable for the customer service experience. Their agency and voice allow them to address inequalities of services, collections, programming, and spaces, and to follow up in order to see that the changes they have called for are implemented, completed, effective, and measured. Empowerment empha-sizes a grassroots advocacy approach and a participatory, people-focused pro-cess for effecting change at library organizational levels.

VOICE

Engaging patrons across your community demographics to participate in an advisory or consulting capacity brings their voices, experiences, and concerns into the library. Feeling heard and seeing problems solved as a result of their advice, opinions, and input creates a sense of ownership in individual patrons and as a collective. Likewise, being heard makes people feel that their opinions and experiences matter and are valued by the library administration. Once library staff train for trauma awareness, their understanding of the symptoms of "problem patrons" as behavioral adaptations, rather than as merely unman-ageable behaviors, allows those patrons' voices to be heard. "Problem patrons" voicing anger, frustration, stress, or anxiety should not be seen as manipu-lative, attention-seeking, or destructive but as people expressing themselves the most effective way that they can.

People belonging to marginalized groups seek and find sanctuary within the library—often, in order to discover the voices and experiences of those like them in memoirs, histories, and works of fiction. Creating opportunities for the marginalized to voice their likes and dislikes and offering them the means to effect change as part of a collective voice representing their identity follows trauma-informed values.

Balancing and including patron voices with those of the library adminis-tration and library workers adheres to trauma-informed principles. Welcom-ing a diversity of perspectives and voices to the conversation about library services, collections, and programs can enrich both our library operations and our communities.

Amelia Anderson (2018) uses the "social model" of disability studies in her work on serving populations with autism in the academic library. The social model says that society is the major contributor to the barriers experienced by people with disabilities. Historically, people with disabilities were excluded from conversations about serving their information needs and providing accessible spaces and collections for them in the planning process. Instead of merely using the Americans with Disabilities Act and applying it to a library space, the library administration should take the additional step of enlisting persons with disabilities for their input about the library and its spaces. One practice is to ask both those familiar with the space and those unfamiliar with it for input about their accessibility experiences in the built library environment. Instead of having someone who is well-abled but wearing mittens walk around your library to test access to doors and buttons and cranks—or any hand-operated device that may present challenges for people with varying abilities—we should solicit people with disabilities who can contribute helpful data about access and accessibility based on their own experience.

For instance, my academic library has an enclosed, card-swipe-accessible study room for graduate students. Another librarian and I were concerned about the weight of the automatically opening door, as well as whether the space was adequate for egress, on top of whether the card-swipe itself was an effective method or not. Our facilities department determined that the automatic door was weighted incorrectly: it was heavier than it should be for anyone to open it, even with the hydraulic assistance built in. Our university's director of disability services met with me and a student who used a motorized wheelchair for mobility. We tested the accessibility of the room, and after much planning and realigning, the student navigated a path to the door and into the room, but required help from me to actively swipe the card to open the door because their arms were affected by hypochondroplasia from birth (short arms and legs).

Just as libraries cannot serve all the needs of all of their patrons, our spaces are bound to fail someone at some point. However, as we listen to patrons' voices and their experiences in our libraries, we can adapt our spaces to increase accessibility within our financial means and within the realm of possibility. Heather Hill's (2013) meta-analysis of the library literature on disability and accessibility found that 25 percent of the articles dealt with accessibility and electronic resources, while 41 percent focused on visual disabilities, with the remainder dealing with motor and other physical disabilities. Unfortunately, Hill also found that librarians were very much occupied by looking at the services and resources offered by libraries, with very few tackling the topic of users' perspectives on making library spaces accessible. With Hill's findings in mind, we should prioritize space accessibility in libraries.

CHOICE

Libraries should offer patrons as many choices as possible in the way they interact with and receive customer service from the library. For instance, how will patrons be contacted when the item they have requested arrives? How will they be contacted about fines? Offering only one method, without allowing patrons to select their preferred medium—text, social media, phone, e-mail, or postcard—alienates individuals and erects communication barriers. For example, patrons in different age demographics can have very different communication preferences. The majority of retired patrons communicate primarily by telephone and U.S. postal mail. Hence, telephone and postcard notifications are the way to reach this age group. Younger patrons' communication preferences range among various options, depending on how tied to technology they are. But generally, e-mail and texting are appropriate communications with them.

Allowing patrons to move furniture to suit their needs is another consideration that a trauma-informed library plans for. Trends in library decor focus on giving patrons more control over seating, studying, standing, or adapting spaces to work for their needs, rather than prescribing their physical behaviors. As a profession, librarianship understands and balances the types of spaces that patrons require in the twenty-first century. Space utilization studies, as well as other methods for collecting data of this type, can identify the busy and quiet parts of library buildings, and these spaces vary in their appeal for people with neurodivergence. Observing patrons' use of spaces and following up with specific questions to individuals, as well as in a focus group setting, can help libraries decide whether a larger or smaller table space is needed. Changing the ambiance is important for all patrons, but especially those with high ACEs. Children, youth, and young adults are more likely to rearrange spaces for group work, or for individual work. For example, one student reported that he prefers backless chairs in the library because they keep him more alert. A chair with a back allows him to slump, and then fall asleep too easily, thus circumventing his purpose of studying, researching, and writing papers in the library. Certain chairs are more comfortable than others, and the use of adaptable furniture that can be pulled apart and combined together serves unspoken needs for control.

Can patrons choose whether to approach library staff to check out materials and pay fines? Or must they only use the self-checkout kiosk for one or more of those tasks? How many options are available to patrons? Giving them as many means as possible to complete the actions they want and need to do within the library is ideal. When patrons have a bad day and need insulation from potential triggers, having self-service technologies so they can avoid person-to-person interaction adds value. On the contrary, for patrons who seek a personal connection, who perhaps ventured out to the library as part of a daily routine in which conversation with another human is a primary goal, having service desks staffed by approachable people can help these patrons fill relational personal goals. Market research demonstrates that millennials prefer experiences, service, and purchases based on positive relationship-building at the outset. They look forward to the relational exchange with each visit. It's likely that most generations feel similarly, since people are universally built for connecting with each other.

At some point it seems that libraries were in the relationship business, in the slower, easier, halcyon days when library staff leisurely read books at the service desks. But given the staff shortages and brisk pace of library services over the past few decades, it seems that customer service in libraries has moved from personal and relational to effective and efficient. When libraries are operated more like businesses and less like human services agencies, relationships aren't encouraged. Library managers encourage those working service desks to serve patrons quickly, and not let the queue of patrons grow longer because they're spending too much time with one patron. When librarians feel constrained at the circulation desk or information desk and are limited in their responses because of directives to move folks along, their authenticity and ability to provide trauma-informed customer service is inhibited. Relationship-building between library staff and patrons has certainly been a casualty of the in-and-out model of customer service.

Theoretically, library staff work directly with people because they're driven by a strong service philosophy which emphasizes human connection and the potential to make a positive difference in their communities. Moreover, driven by millennials' preferences for relationship-building, libraries have tended to create service desks where consistency and continuity are available. Millennial patrons want to see service desks staffed by familiar faces. And in fact, all generations do. This was the case when I worked at a small rural public library. The retired patrons there, who belonged to the traditionalist generation, appreciated their relationship with me as I provided customer service, reader's advisory, community referrals, and warm personal exchanges.

What choices do we offer regarding privacy? How often is patrons' privacy violated because of the technological shifts in information discovery? How committed is the library to setting limits on the online tracking and surveillance of our patrons' information-seeking habits by outside interests? Library discovery tools are designed so that they discard borrowing records, since this level of patron privacy is a well-established foundation of library systems. However, patrons' online use behaviors are actively tracked, and theoretically are used to improve the user experience. Our online environment prevents libraries from controlling the privacy risks that patrons encounter when using our discovery systems, websites, and Wi-Fi for the transmission of information. Often the fight over patron privacy pits public service librarians against systems librarians. While we both have the best interests of our patrons in mind, our philosophies of service, notions of privacy, and methods in pursuing our objectives are often at odds with each other. The librarians and staff who work with our integrated library systems (ILS) can be less sensitive to privacy concerns because they're data junkies and are prone to assess services based on the copious data they've amassed. Library staff with computer science backgrounds can be unsympathetic to librarianship's Code of Ethics, which values patron privacy. Some librarians lack customer service skills or emotional intelligence skills and prefer working with data and software as opposed to people and their information needs. Hence, they may scoff at the notion of patron privacy when information tools can yield vast amounts of granular data on patron behavior in order to improve the user experience through website design and database retrieval. Ultimately, our goal is to strengthen the experience of choice within our ILS and remove barriers to access. However, with each new ILS release, it's been my experience that our systems insert multiple steps before reaching our goals, whether they be online access or interlibrary loan. The more barriers our ILS assemble within the process, the more complex and frustrating it becomes for patrons. The irony is that we promote efficiency in our person-to-person services, while creating inefficiencies with online access because of multiple requirements to log in and authenticate affiliations. Offering library patrons choices to opt in or out of data collection (while providing a link to the library's privacy statement, which provides a means for informed consent) while they use discovery tools is a trauma-informed practice.

Given this, we need to recognize and validate our patrons' strengths. We teach them new skills like how to search our databases and how to refine their search terms. Library staffers work as partners in collaboration with each patron. That's why two of the most important questions within the reference interview involve time. First, asking "How much time do you have for me to help you with your question?" provides scope and context for the next five to fifty minutes. Second, asking about the patron's deadline for the information, "When do you need this? May I get back to you tomorrow?" helps us determine whether to teach patrons about filtering aspects when it comes to full text or whether they have time for the interlibrary loan process. Trauma-informed libraries aim to strengthen library staff, patrons, and community members' experience of choice. We recognize that every patron's library experience is distinctive, and this requires an ever-changing individualized approach to customer service in which we meet the patron where they are with our best abilities. Trauma-informed libraries believe in the resilience of individuals and communities and their ability to heal and recover from trauma. We build upon the skills and experiences that patrons possess instead of responding to their perceived shortfalls, such as limited domain knowledge.

Empowerment does not happen by chance. It is chosen by the leadership and the library administration. Sharing power is an integral part of trauma-informed services. This shared-power relationship eschews compliance for learning. This learning model is what supports and encourages enduring change.

10

Cultural, Historical, and Gender Issues

Another component of trauma-informed care involves cultural, historical and gender issues. This, in effect, is libraries tweaking their customer services, collections, and outreach events to move past cultural stereotypes and the biases of the profession. Developing new service models or adapting old ones with an emphasis on removing their bias, is appropriate. Examining collections for problematic labels, cataloging, or metadata and actively using alternative subject headings that are inclusive and don't promote colonialism, sexism, racism, or homophobia are ways to make improvements in this area.

Some initial questions to ask are: Are the services offered by the library gender-responsive? Is the library leveraging the healing value of traditional cultural connections? Is the library just checking off boxes on the surface, but not actually realigning its practices for inclusion? An example of this is only offering or featuring LGBTQ-related exhibits, bibliographies, and programs in June during Pride Month. But trauma-informed and culturally competent libraries should promote LGBTQ resources, collections, and programs all through the year. The same can be said for similarly designated months, like Black History Month (February), Women's History Month (March), and Native American History Month (November). Admittedly, having these designated months does make planning for exhibits and programs easier. But we shouldn't limit these initiatives to four weeks of each year, since patrons with marginalized identities can become more integral to our library outreach, programming, and exhibits year-round. Lastly, trauma-informed libraries need to recognize and address historical trauma.

CULTURAL ISSUES

Cultural issues call for the library staff and administration to consider the diversity of patrons' values and beliefs about knowledge, information, community, and free speech. Cultural issues include areas like race, ethnicity, immigration status, sexuality, urbanity and rurality, and disability. Trauma-informed libraries recognize the systematic effects that inequity has upon minority or marginalized groups and then try to address the specific needs of individuals belonging to those groups. Cultural awareness, responsiveness, and empathy are essential for increasing access to information and library services, as well as for lessening the chance of re-traumatization for children, families, and communities. Eliminating disparities from library services requires a culturally responsive mindset on the part of both the administration and staff.

One strategy for increasing your library's sensitivity to cultural issues is to ask patrons questions and then listen to their answers. Ask library patrons what worries them the most. Ask patrons how they feel about using outside referral and resources. Treat patrons with respect. Adapting the ESFT Model, which is used in health and human services agencies, for use in libraries can be helpful here. E denotes the Explanatory model of information: What kind of library help do you think you need? S is Social and environmental factors: How do you get information? How do you access information? What transportation can you use to visit the library? Do you have help getting to the library? F is Fears and concerns: Does this information/resource/book seem okay to you? Are you concerned about its biases, credibility, accuracy, authority? T is Therapeutic contracting: Do you understand how to apply this information to your problem? Can you tell me how you'll cite the information (if needed)?

Another consideration that library staff should keep in mind when providing culturally sensitive customer services is to view relationships through the trauma-informed framework. You should understand your role as an information provider for the patron and try to gain a better understanding of how the patron intends to use the information. You should also consider including others when helping a library patron. In my reference and research coterie, we regularly invite librarians into our offices when we're consulting with students, especially when we know that our colleagues have knowledge or networks from which we can draw in helping students. Librarians working with youth should consider including their parents or siblings in the process so that any imprecise language or instructions used by the librarians can be explained in language they recognize and understand. When working with more than one patron, librarians should consider the group's resources and the barriers to help-seeking from library staff. Examples include working with ESL learners. Having a native English speaker to assist these learners in the library is a good practice. People with intellectual disabilities often have a friend or family member accompanying them, and library workers should address both people so that clarity is experienced, and miscommunication is alleviated.

Nicola Andrews (2018) instructs librarians in practicing cultural humility. Cultural humility is an open-ended process of empathy and understanding as demonstrated by library workers. Andrews outlines three main concepts: examining and understanding your own background, committing to dismantle and redress power structures, and building relationships. She explains that practicing and projecting cultural humility is difficult for people who cling to their identity as an expert or authority. Training library staff around cultural humility can be tough, since building trust around issues of race remains difficult in our cultural institutions. Many people avoid discussions of race because they are uncomfortable, they "don't see color," or they are enmeshed within white fragility. Part of the library staff training in trauma-informed care includes exercises spent developing a shared language around race and culture so that everyone clearly communicates and can resolve issues related to bias and preconceptions. Being nice, keeping the peace, and not wanting to say the wrong thing can keep library staff from getting real when it comes to race. The library administration should be very transparent about the difficulties we can expect when talking about race, trauma, and culture and their effects on customer services. The administration should acknowledge that everyone makes mistakes, but that we are learning to move forward in TIC customer services.

Trauma is usually retained psychologically within a cultural context like mass incarceration, poverty, or being a first-generation high school or college student. Library staff are better equipped to provide trauma-informed customer service when they pay attention to the underlying and systemic causes of cultural issues. You should encourage library staff who are interested in cultural humility to form a book club so that conversations around issues of culture, oppression, race, and trauma have a normalized, buttressed role within the library. And that conversations around cultural issues are normalized as part of library operations.

HISTORICAL ISSUES

Recognizing and understanding the effects that historical, multigenerational trauma or institutional trauma have had on our service populations is necessary for successful trauma-informed approaches. This differs from the cultural issues discussed previously, which focus on individuals, because historical issues allow libraries, as institutions, to scrutinize how their systems and organizational structures have traumatized or re-traumatize these communities. The emphasis on historical issues here involves institutional change. Some questions to ask are: How have our practices and policies created unsafe, isolating libraries? And once we've examined and updated our practices, how do we align them with the trauma-informed framework?

Those familiar with the history of our profession and our libraries understand the kinds of issues and dynamics we've consciously worked to address and solve. Private, subscription libraries and free public libraries emerged in American cities as early as 1711, with one in Boston. A tax-supported library opened in Peterborough, New Hampshire, in 1833. These early public libraries served white people. Prior to the Civil War, education was systematically denied to both enslaved and free blacks in almost all the Southern states. After the Civil War, churches, schools, and other benevolent organizations worked to educate African American citizens, but over half of the black population in the United States still couldn't read. However, the Philadelphia Library Company of Colored Persons had been founded in 1833 by Robert Purvis, and from 1828 to 1928 more than fifty African American literary societies and libraries were founded in Northern cities to serve the need.

During Reconstruction (1865–77), African Americans in the South enjoyed a short period in which they could vote, hold elected office, seek their own employment, enjoy access to public services, and exercise other basic civil rights. After Reconstruction ended, Southern blacks' political power declined and their economic condition deteriorated, and in 1896 the *Plessy v. Ferguson* decision by the U.S. Supreme Court established the "separate but equal" provision characterizing the Jim Crow era. In the era of strict racial segregation and discrimination that followed, African Americans in the South were barred from white schools and churches, and were barred altogether from using public libraries and many other facilities. For example, the new public library built in Atlanta, Georgia, in 1902 excluded African Americans. W. E. B. DuBois publicly opposed that prohibition, but the first Atlanta library branch offering services to African Americans didn't open until 1921. The first public library for African Americans that was staffed solely by them was a branch of the Louisville Free (KY) Public Library, which opened in 1905. *Plessy v. Ferguson* was overturned in 1954, but many public libraries in the South resisted integration until the Civil Rights Act of 1964 outlawed segregation in public facilities and banned employment discrimination based on race, color, religion, sex, or national origin.

Those of us lacking lived experiences of segregation and the Civil Rights Movement in the mid-twentieth century take the availability of library services to all for granted. But the film *Hidden Figures* (2016), based on the lives and experiences of African American women working at NASA to launch the astronaut John Glenn into orbit in 1962, contains a scene depicting an African American woman approached by a librarian who says, "We don't want any trouble in here" and directs her, and her two sons, to the "colored section," which doesn't include the books the woman needs. When the woman objects, the librarian responds, "That's just the way it is," and the next scene shows a white male police officer escorting the woman and her sons out of the library. Despite this film's depiction of unsympathetic librarians in the South at this time, Freedom Libraries sprang up in more than eighty locations in the Deep South as part of the Civil Rights Movement. For example, the Selma (AL) Free Library, staffed by volunteers, offered donated books and other materials to the city's African Americans and gave them access to a library for the first time.

Libraries have had a complicated history of institutionalized racism. John Hope Franklin, an African American historian, documented his disquieting experiences in North Carolina archival collections in his 1963 essay "The Dilemma of the American Negro Scholar." Actively working to overcome that legacy is imperative, especially in our supposedly "post-racial" culture. Ashley Farmer (2018) writes about how archives marginalize black scholars and stresses the importance of examining the biases built into the systems and infrastructure of archives. She says that black scholars and students are viewed by archives staff as anomalies and threats. At my own university, I was told by several students of color that one archives staffer made them feel unsafe, distrusted, and surveilled in our archives. From the time they were asked for identification, to filling out researcher paperwork, to asking for manuscripts and receiving them, the staffer's tone and manner toward them was hostile, curt, and let them know they were unwelcome in the space. The students reported being surveilled constantly as they completed their assignment for class. Clearly, this was not my own experience with the archives staff because I am white, and they knew me from our working in the same building, as well from my use of the archives for professional research.

Ethlene Whitmire (2004) studied campus racial climates and undergraduates' perceptions of the academic library. She suggested that African American students may experience microaggressions in academic libraries. Whitmire's earlier studies indicated that African American students asked for help more frequently than white students, but that their experiences were not very different from each other. She also cites work by Feagin, Vera, and Imain (1996), who identify "white spaces" on campuses where students of color don't feel welcome. However, these researchers found that the academic library wasn't considered a white space. Elijah Anderson originated the concept of "white spaces," which are characterized as being informally off-limits public places in which blacks are unexpected, marginalized, or otherwise absent.

Given the history of racism in the United States, both individual and institutionalized, it is understandable that African Americans and other disenfranchised groups may view libraries of all types as white spaces and white institutions, and either approach them with caution or avoid them altogether. If you recall from chapter 7, the teenaged black girl's major trigger was older white women. African Americans and other people of color carry a historic distrust of white people and our institutions. In chapter 6, Daniel Day's example of indifferent record-keeping by city officials was mentioned as an example of institutionalized racism that he and his family experienced. At another point in his memoir, he wrote about never working with white designers—he is a fashion designer who came to prominence in the early 1990s—because of his complete distrust of white people, which he attributes to the promise made by the U.S. government to give freed Southern blacks forty acres and the use of army mules, a promise that was annulled by President Andrew Johnson.

GENDER ISSUES

The "father" of our profession, Melvil Dewey, was an inveterate sexual harasser who touched, hugged, and kissed female acquaintances to the extent that women with whom he worked brought lawsuits against him for his indecent behavior. He was a racist, too, and wouldn't admit Jews or African Americans to the private resort he owned and operated at Lake Placid, New York. From the start, librarianship has dealt with inappropriate behavior, mostly from a library staff point of view. The majority of library work is performed by staffers who are women. But male staffers disproportionately occupy positions of authority and leadership. Male library leaders are rarely on the front lines of customer service, and this places the burden of policy enforcement on the (largely female) staff who must work directly with poorly behaving patrons. And these are the same library staff who, in some cases, lack the autonomy to protect themselves and are inhibited by procedural guidelines from doing so. Library staff must inevitably deal with unsavory behavior from offensive patrons. Most female and non-binary, queer, and trans library staffers can share stories about creepy male patrons who leer, stand too close, stare at their bodies, and generally create a hostile work environment by abusing the power they hold in the "customer is always right" type of service model. In these instances, library staff lack empowerment, voice, and choice—the basic tenets of trauma-informed approaches to library customer services. They are disempowered by library policies which insist that they remain professional and neutral, and politely deflect inappropriate comments. The expectation from the library administration is that library staff should remain polite and helpful, even as they're being emotionally assaulted. They aren't allowed to authoritatively demand that the offensive patron leave the building. Nor do they have many choices of how best to diffuse the situation and negotiate a resolution. And if library staff don't present enough of a captive audience for harassers, these inappropriate men also harass fellow library patrons who are girls or women. And if library staff are unable—for whatever reason—to respond effectively to the harassment by shutting it down, the harasser feels free to continue their bad behavior. Many libraries have security personnel on their premises to deal effectively with these situations as they arise.

Previously, we've talked about how libraries provide sanctuary and privacy, are recognized as neutral organizations, and function as safe spaces for everyone. Libraries are places where young writers come to spend time, and they're also places where young LGBTQ people can discover freedom for themselves. One notable example of this is the writer James Baldwin, a gay black man who spent much of his adolescence in Harlem's libraries in the 1930s and 1940s. Actively creating safe zones within our libraries for LBGTQ children, tweens, teens, and adults is a central aim of trauma-informed approaches to library customer services. In fact, "calm zones" or "safe zones" are part and parcel of TIC classrooms at the K–12 level. Children in TIC classrooms can easily access these calm/safe zones when they're feeling anxious. These spaces are typically in their assigned classroom, but they offer some privacy and allow children to play with objects that will calm them down, or simply sit there quietly and breathe, so that they can return to the classroom activity with a fresh, calmed mind. These spaces closely parallel the types of environments that public and school libraries have provided for decades.

LGBTQ youth are at risk and are unsafe in our communities, our schools, our churches, and our libraries. While the younger generation tends to more readily accept LGBTQ people than members of older generations do, hatred-fueled violence against LGBTQ youth does occur, often on a wide scale. Data from 2001 indicated that 38 percent of LGBTQ youth were physically harassed because of their sexual orientation. More alarmingly, high school youth with these marginalized identities are three times more likely to attempt suicide or self-harm than their straight friends. And about half of all transgender youth have seriously considered suicide.

There are many ways to physically indicate that the library is a safe area. (See chapter 5 on safety and review it for ideas.) The National Education Association offers safe zone posters for classrooms. These may be appropriate for school libraries and others, depending on their messaging and context. Other types of libraries can easily design posters appropriate for their space and populations.

Julie Ann Winkelstein identified several barriers to serving LGBTQ teens and adults in public libraries in her 2012 dissertation. The majority of barriers lay in librarians' attitudes. Librarians claimed that finding materials for this group was too difficult; they felt personally uncomfortable with LGBTQ materials; or they simply believed that the materials didn't belong in their library. Another belief of the librarians studied by Winkelstein was that only heterosexuals used their library. The librarians' answers demonstrated a complete lack of awareness and empathy as professionals who purport to observe the Code of Ethics.

Library staffers' tone of voice, volume, eye contact, and body language can also help to create safe spaces for LGBTQ people. According to Beth Berila (2011), LGBTQ people constantly read their environment for its level of safety. Once they understand the level of safety in an environment, or in a group of library staff or among other library patrons, they position their identity in relation to that space. Berila talks about how LGBTQ youth demonstrate survival skills by carefully reading the climate and then adapting their expression, body language, and so on according to the situation or space they are in. They scan the environment and then check in with themselves for any people, words, or feelings that raise their antennae or that raise a red flag. They feel safest in spaces that don't raise their antennae. Green flags are all go, where they can physically and mentally relax. However, being vigilant about every public space is mentally, emotionally, and physically exhausting. Making LGBTQ people feel welcome takes commitment and extended effort.

Many people use the term *red flag* to denote a warning or a danger signal. For example, a red flag for library job candidates may occur during the interview process when they ask about the onboarding plan or schedule. If the search committee responds with a non-answer or indicates that there is no onboarding plan, this is a red flag; the candidate may conclude that the library lacks a commitment to training and orientation, and hence they will be more likely to decline a job offer from that library. We have all had bad experiences in workplaces and in all kinds of relationships. We learn from those experiences and are attuned to negative or potentially distressing signs when we're interviewing with new libraries or going on first dates with potential mates. For example, in the situation described above, the candidate had learned from a previous job that a supervisor who schedules personal leave time for themselves during the new hire's first week and does not organize and schedule work for them, correlated to a latter pattern of thoughtlessness, ineffectiveness, and narcissism on the supervisor's part. The environmental signs discussed in earlier chapters are the red, yellow, and green flags that tell LGBTQ people whether they are safe and where others' level of commitment to their safety is situated. Yellow flags may be of concern, but if they occur singly, they are not at the red flag level. However, multiple yellow flags may equal a red flag.

Students at ETSU look for indications that the staff and faculty are "safe zone" graduates. Our university has a community of LGBTQ allies who've attended training and signed a pledge of commitment to a variety of items. They affix a sign or magnet to their door to indicate that LGBTQ people are welcome and safe there. They affirm their commitment to fighting heterosexism and homophobia on campus and in our broader community. They believe that the campus community is enriched by the presence of LGBTQ people. They make everyone feel safe on campus. They are visible and nonjudgmental supporters. They self-educate. They refer LGBTQ students to both on- and off-campus resources. For other types of libraries, displaying the rainbow flag or other symbols may increase feelings of safety.

When planning for and providing gender-responsive services, library administrators should make sure that the assessment instruments they use have been designed for or tested with both women and men before considering them reliable, credible, and unbiased. Treating all library patrons as individuals rather than resorting to gendered stereotypes and traditions when providing customer service is a basic responsibility.

The library administration should review the reporting process for sexual harassment so that the management configuration doesn't reinforce abuses of power or maladjusted gender dynamics. In hierarchical libraries with many layers, letting library staff skip their immediate supervisor (if they are the problem or are complicit) and go up at least one level or two, may assuage potential abuses of power or imbalances in gender dynamics. Another option is turning to your organization's human resources office, where complaints can be addressed by potentially impartial individuals who have the authority to see that justice is done. It is the library administration's responsibility to clarify and communicate its behavior policies and enforce them by holding violators accountable and providing consequences for abuses.

Potential problems with these gender issues, as well as others mentioned in this chapter, can arise when the library administration lacks emotional intelligence or is otherwise indifferent to human suffering. Some library directors, K–12 principals, and deans will not take responsibility for setting the tone or modeling the behavior they want reflected in library staffers' actions. In some instances, they may blame the problem on the library staffer who has lodged a complaint and use gaslighting techniques to absolve themselves from accountability. For example, they may imply that the staffer is oversensitive or has misinterpreted someone's tone or meaning. Instead of working to solve the problem and create a healthy, neutral work environment, an ineffective leadership blames the victim and suggests that they remove themselves from spaces, meetings, or service areas in which they feel unsafe or threatened.

Normalized gender harassment, or other inappropriate behaviors such as bullying, mobbing, or freezing out coworkers, may be difficult to address or change if the library's culture has allowed those behaviors to flourish. Library staff with traumatic family histories or domestic violence experiences can keenly identify dysfunctional work environments and can be valuable for serving, in effect, as canaries in the mine. On the other hand, these survivors' inappropriate behaviors in the workplace may be normalized because the organizational climate mirrors the dysfunction of their own childhood home.

RECOGNIZING AND ADDRESSING HISTORICAL TRAUMA

Examples of historical trauma include genocide, slavery, forced relocation, and the destruction of cultural practices. The term *historical trauma* is often used by historians, social workers, and psychologists; it originated in the 1960s to describe the experiences of the children of Holocaust survivors. The term has expanded to include numerous Indigenous groups globally that have shared histories of colonization or oppression, as well as people with histories of ethnic cleansing, forced relocation, incarceration, victimization, or considerable group trauma contact. The term *considerable group trauma* includes our military, as well as first responders like law enforcement officers, emergency medical technicians, and firefighters. It also includes gang members who have lost multiple members to death and serious injury. There are three elements involved in historical trauma: a traumatic event, the shared experience of the event by the group, and the multigenerational effect of the trauma. Populations with historically experienced mass trauma tend to have a higher incidence of chronic diseases in subsequent generations. Studies suggest that the children of Holocaust survivors, ranging from Israel to Canada, are more susceptible to PTSD and display heightened symptoms of this disorder.

While the transgenerational effect of the Holocaust on subsequent generations remains controversial, the evidence does suggest that shared traumatic experiences can result in cumulative emotional and psychological wounds that span generations of affected communities. The traumas inflicted and experienced due to ethnicity, race, or creed remain within the collective psyche, which in turn can result in a higher incidence of mental and physical illness, chronic diseases, substance abuse and addiction, and the attrition of families and community structures and supports. These cycles of historical trauma are difficult to escape, because while the experiences were in the past, their effects remain in the present.

Some more familiar examples include the historical traumas experienced by American Indians and Alaska Natives (AIAN), Jews during the Holocaust, and African Americans during slavery. People belonging to groups who experienced historical trauma tend to distrust outsiders and the government because of their long-term negative experiences with these parties. For AIANs, the effects of violent colonization during the past three centuries have resulted in a complete breakdown of traditional AIAN values. As a result, alcoholism and substance abuse and addiction are normalized and prevalent within their communities. AIANs' rates of depression, anxiety, and suicidality are proportionally higher than other groups of Americans. Child abuse, neglect, and domestic violence are also endemic in many AIAN communities, as is the incidence of PTSD. Due to the loss of their traditional way of life, AIANs struggle with a lack of meaning and purpose in their lives. Consequently, there is little hope that their families' lives will improve during their lifetime or in the future. They battle internalized oppression and self-hatred via insidious cultural messages from popular culture, the media, and historic government-sponsored education, policies, and programs that were aimed at "killing the Indian and saving the man," practices whose focus was the assimilation of Indians into the mainstream of white settler society.

Historical trauma is expressed in three ways. First, there is unresolved grief that may not have been acknowledged, addressed thoroughly, or expressed. Second, there is the failure of the dominant white culture to understand the losses AIANs suffered in the past due to settler-colonialism, epidemic disease, and forced reeducation. Lastly, there is the internalized racism that AIANs absorb by internalizing the oppressor's perspective, which results in an endless cycle of self-hatred that finds expression in self-harm and negative behaviors.

MICROAGGRESSIONS

Microaggressions are brief and commonplace verbal, nonverbal, or environmental indignities that communicate an insult toward someone, but specifically to members of marginalized groups. Chester M. Pierce coined the term *microaggressions* in the late 1960s and used it to describe a racial dynamic that white Americans perpetuated upon black Americans. However, in the past five decades, the term and the practices it labels have expanded to include all persons who are members of marginalized groups.

Environmental microaggressions often occur in libraries. Library buildings, collections, and rooms named after white, heterosexual, upper-class men are an environmental microaggression, as are all-white male administrations in K–12 schools, academic libraries, and the boards in public libraries. The lack of representation of marginalized groups throughout the library's collections, programming, and staffing is another form of microaggression. And of course, libraries that are hostile and invalidating to certain patrons (and library staff) are another example.

Microaggressions are usually covert and subtle; they are not the typical outright racism that many people can easily identify when they see, hear, or experience it. Sometimes the ambiguity of a microaggression leaves the target of the behavior with stress, anxiety, discomfort, and uncertainty of how to respond. African Americans report more of these experiences than other groups. Some people believe that microaggressions are imagined due to the oversensitivity of the person reporting the occurrence, or that people who experience microaggressions are neurotic. Gaslighters typically tell people they're oversensitive or imagining things. And white people, with no lived experience of racism, are often blind to microaggressions. Typical microaggressions by white people include confusing people of color with each other. Elaine Welteroth (2019), former editor-in-chief of *Teen Vogue*, related her experience as one of two African American women working at a magazine. Her white colleagues regularly confused Elaine's and the other woman's name because all they saw were interchangeable women of color, not individuals.

In her 2015 article "Racial Microaggressions in Academic Libraries: Results of a Survey of Minority and Non-Minority Librarians," Jaena Alabi concluded that white librarians rarely recognize racial microaggressions in personal exchanges for what they are. By contrast, academic librarians of color reported that they are treated differently from their white colleagues. Alabi suggests the possibility that racial microaggressions are part of what keeps the ranks of academic librarians 86 percent white.

Joy Doan and Ahmed Alwan (2017) use the idea of microaggressions to frame the experiences that library faculty encounter from "teaching faculty" at the same institution. Doan and Alwan state that teaching faculty tend to treat library faculty as inferiors, not as colleagues or collaborators. Their study determined that some microaggressions exist but concluded that the problem may be librarianship's perception as a service, or as a subordinate identity within higher education.

When white people make a big deal about pronouncing people of color's names with statements like "That's an unusual name," that's a microaggression. Telling an Asian person that you were "shanghaied" into doing something is a microaggression. Asking Jewish library staff to create a display, bibliography, or LibGuide on the Holocaust is a microaggression. Asking male-identified people to move and lift heavy furniture, books, and other objects in the library is a microaggression. Misgendering people is a microaggression. Refusing anyone's request to call them by their gendered pronoun of choice is also a microaggression. People with unseen or invisible disabilities may encounter librarians who disregard their requests for accommodations. Dress policies that ban hoodies and sagging pants, thus targeting African American males, are microaggressions. Comments and jokes about race, gender, ability, and sexual identity or orientation are both micro- and macro-aggressions. When a person with a disability joins a meeting and someone says, "We heard you coming" because of their cane/wheelchair/brace, that is a microaggression. Library staff who have had mandated diversity training but still create Christmas-themed events and programs for the library are practicing microaggressions.

Stock microaggression phrases are: "You sound too educated to be . . ." Or "_____ can speak more on that topic since they are _____." More examples are documented on the lismicroagggressions Tumblr. While most library staff know how to find information and refer patrons to others who may be of more help than they are, refusing to educate ourselves on general topics of interest to our diverse populations is not okay. Practicing inclusion and equity means keeping up with the times and learning everyone's preferred forms of identity. Unfortunately, library staff who commit microaggressions are often unaware that their behavior is offensive; it's likely that they believe they're displaying empathy, when in fact they're doing the opposite. They have no idea how their words and actions are actually affecting colleagues and patrons.

Phoebe Robinson (2016) recounts the microaggressions she experienced during a customer service failure at Michael's, the crafts supply store, in her memoir *You Can't Touch My Hair: And Other Things I Still Have to Explain*. She was the first person waiting in line at the framing desk in her local Michael's store. There were two Michael's clerks available, but neither one of them welcomed or acknowledged her when she arrived at the service desk, nor did they until ten minutes passed and they had helped two other white customers instead of her. She spoke up and finally received service. Does this happen at your library's service counters? If so, correct it.

Furthermore, Robinson talks about how women of color, after experiencing racism—either macro- or microaggressions—often don't say anything about it because they don't want to be perceived as an "angry black woman." Additionally, Robinson says there are times when black women must make people aware that what they said or did is offensive. When people aren't called out for their words, actions, or behaviors, they cannot self-reflect and change. Moreover, when people being called out for racism or microaggressions accuse the one calling them out of being too sensitive, angry, or out to make everything about race, that is gaslighting.

Library patrons who absorb microaggressions from library staff feel invisible, discounted, disrespected, powerless, and unsafe within the library. Library staff who experience microaggressions from their patrons, colleagues, or the administration experience the same feelings, but those states of mind spread and affect the integrity of the library's morale and efficiency, and ultimately affect our ability to provide adequate levels of customer service. Microaggressions also deny equal access and opportunity in both education and employment, which are codified by American laws.

Library staff can be allies by not participating in others' microaggressions, by educating themselves, and by disrupting any microaggressive behavior and supporting the target. Professional development in the form of workshops is one method of introducing the topic to library workers.

For library workers who experience microaggressions, they should ask themselves a few questions to determine what actions, or non-actions, to take when faced with the experience:

- If I respond, could my physical safety be in danger?
- If I respond, will the person become defensive, and will this lead to an argument?
- If I respond, how will this affect my relationship with this person?
- If I don't respond, will I regret not saying anything?
- If I don't respond, does that convey my acceptance of the behavior or statement?

Some may choose passive-aggressive ways of responding, such as eye-rolling, teeth-sucking, or sighing. Others may feel that calling out microaggressions is therapeutic, especially if there are years of accumulated anger and frustration. For example, when a black man notices that a white woman flinches and tucks her purse closer as she sees him enter the elevator, or as he passes by her on the sidewalk, this reminds him of racial stereotypes and is a microaggression.

More assertive library workers may pause and ask the offender, "What did you mean by that?" This also lets the person correct their mistake. Library workers can calmly address how the behavior made them feel with language like "I felt hurt when you said _____." Library workers may choose to

educate the perpetrator about the offense, but others are tired of functioning in that role for clueless white people. Another strategy is to address the
behavior and not the person: "Your behavior is racially and sexually charged
and offensive." The writer and feminist Audre Lorde said:

> For in order to survive, those of us for whom oppression is as
> American as apple pie have always had to be watchers, to become
> familiar with the language and the manners of the oppressor, even
> sometimes adopting them for some illusion of protection. When-
> ever the need for some pretense of communication arises, those
> who profit from our oppression call upon us to share our knowl-
> edge with them. . . . In other words, it is the responsibility of the
> oppressed to teach the oppressors their mistakes. I am responsi-
> ble for educating teachers who dismiss my children's culture in
> school. Black and Third World people are expected to educate
> white people as to our humanity. Women are expected to educate
> men. Lesbians and gay men are expected to educate the hetero-
> sexual world. The oppressors maintain their position and evade
> responsibility for their own actions. There is a constant drain of
> energy which might be better used in redefining ourselves and
> devising realistic scenarios for altering the present and construct-
> ing the future. (Lorde 1984)

Sometimes we may inadvertently microaggress someone. When this happens, own up to it and apologize to the person. Listen and try not to be defensive. Invalidating their hurt feelings is also a microaggression. Be aware of the
language that you use in this interaction. Don't add insult to injury by saying,
"That's so lame."

Library administrators must demonstrate that they are committed to
change the organizational culture by educating staff and clearly defining
what local actions can be taken to minimize the microaggressions anyone in
the library experiences. The administration's obligations in this area include
addressing any incidents of microaggression and other injustices in the library
and investigating them quickly, sensitively, and as thoroughly as possible.
Library staff and library patrons breaking the policies should be held accountable and receive disciplinary action.

We can establish supportive communities and patron-driven initiatives
that may have a positive effect on the library, community, or campus climate.
A useful guide is the Inclusive Excellence Toolkit by Jesus Trevino, Thomas
Walker, and Johanna Leyba of Denver University's Center for Multicultural
Excellence (www.du.edu/cme). While its primary audience is higher education,
the toolkit can be modified and used by libraries of all types that are interested
in exploring, applying, and entrenching inclusiveness within their organization.

PART III

Creating a Culture of Trauma-Informed Care in Libraries

11

Assessing Organizational Readiness

How can a library administration know if their library is receptive to making trauma-informed changes to operations and organizational culture? The library leadership cannot know if the library staff is receptive to change unless they spend time and energy evaluating the organization's readiness for the transformation. Conducting a self-study prior to embarking upon organizational change will help the administration identify key areas that are in need of work and study. Once data from the readiness evaluation has been analyzed, any recommendations stemming from that process are evidence-based and will be significantly more likely to increase success. Also, this process may save time and effort in the long run, especially if the organization is not ready, or will ever be ready, for changes such as these.

LAYING THE GROUNDWORK

Additionally, libraries need to tailor the implementation of trauma-informed approaches to their specific system and resources. The first step, of course, is to educate the library's staff and stakeholders about the basics of trauma and adverse childhood experiences, how these may well affect a majority of our population, and why tweaking our customer service models in a trauma-informed direction will pay off in the long term for everyone. With minimal implementation, libraries can review and revise their policies and practices, as well as identify ways to make their spaces safer for both library staff and library patrons.

A second-level implementation requires acknowledging that a significant cultural change must occur for authentic and fully charged trauma-informed practices to pay off for library patrons and library workers. Individually working with library units to translate trauma-informed practices into their workflow is possible at this level of implementation. At this stage, libraries have an opportunity to examine and remove any visible and invisible barriers to the adoption of trauma-informed practices. As more in-depth training occurs, library workers' awareness of the effects of trauma on our patrons' lives, as well as on our own, deepens.

Those libraries that are fully committed to trauma-informed care become part of a trauma-informed learning network in their communities and in the profession. Library staff can identify organizational and professional progress and grow their capacity for trauma-informed customer services. Staff training and learning about trauma should become the norm within the organization. The peer support networks for both library patrons and staff should be robust and valuable.

Trauma-informed changes are medium-sized in scope. These changes affect both the organization and individual workers; primarily, library staff who work closely with library patrons. But these changes also have the potential to affect library staff behind the scenes, since changes to websites, ILS, and technology may be required as well. Trauma-informed changes can affect processes, organization, and job roles and may be used strategically to bolster customer services. Thus, embarking on this framework may require a great deal of effort from some libraries, and a minimal amount from others. Hence, the importance of planning your change strategy.

Assessing the library's readiness invokes our curiosity and compels constant questioning. What do you know about your library's culture and value system? Once you understand the answer, it's possible to predict what questions, reactions, and resistance will crop up, and effectively neutralize them. How can the library's capacity for change be measured? How effective were changes made in the past? Are there historical obstacles or personal beliefs preventing change? Do these obstacles consist of people, beliefs, processes, or systems? What organizational baggage does the library retain from past changes? The timing may never be right in certain libraries because organizations have a limited capacity for change, and likewise, library staff have varying levels of resilience and ability to roll with the punches. How will middle managers in the library process this change? Are they allied with the library administration, or with the library staff? How resilient are the library staff? How possible is change?

Furthermore, what is the library leadership's management style, and how is power distributed, or not distributed? Where do informal or unaccount-ed-for pockets of power and potential resistance exist? And a better question: why do those pockets of resistance exist? Getting those individuals, or teams, on board is essential for making this type of change, or any kind of change that will be effective over the long term. The most important aspects of man-aging changes in libraries are the staff's perception of these changes, their individual personal readiness for change in general, and their belief or lack of belief in trauma-informed approaches' potential effectiveness for improved customer service.

Understanding what's in it for them can help counter resistance from the staff. Perhaps the change will support their professional goals. Or maybe knowing that the change will not put their jobs at risk will dissolve any resis-tance they might have. Can exposure to the trauma-informed framework affect their families in a positive way? What's the probability that the change will positively affect library workers' health and well-being? And what's the likeli-hood that this type of change will result in a more positive work environment?

SELF-ASSESSMENT

Asking and answering eight questions either "yes" or "no" can determine how well-equipped the library administration is for adopting a trauma-informed approach in the organization:

1. Is the need for trauma-informed care in the organization clearly defined?
2. Is this organizational model appropriate for our library?
3. Is the timing right for this initiative?
4. Will library leaders support this change and the effort required to implement and sustain trauma-informed approaches?
5. Will the library provide library workers with adequate time and resources to support active project participation?
6. Will the library allow time to prepare and consistently work on trauma-informed principles?
7. Will the library measure and assess progress and remain committed to continuous improvement?
8. Will the library reinforce and reward positive behaviors and improvements within the trauma-informed framework?

Using the yes/no answers to these eight questions gives an immediate response to the organization's readiness and commitment to change. If you answered "yes" to less than three of the questions, now is not the time for change. Change attempted at this time will likely fail. Instead, you should focus on raising the readiness level of your library. Guides for organizational read-iness for change are accessible via Internet search engines. If you answered "yes" to 4 or 5 of the questions, then your library is only partially ready, and the likelihood of paradigm change is low. If you answered "yes" to 6–8 of the questions, then your library is more likely to have success with implementing a trauma-informed model for customer services.

There are several readiness surveys and questionnaires that the library administration can use to poll library workers. Many are available free online, and a simple search for "change readiness assessment," "community readiness model," or "agency self-assessment" in a search engine will return many results.

The National Center on Family Homelessness's Trauma-Informed Organizational Toolkit contains a survey instrument that libraries can adapt for their purposes. Sections include supporting staff development, creating a safe and supportive environment, assessing and planning services, involving customers, and adapting policies. The toolkit is freely available from the American Institute of Research's website: www.air.org/resource/trauma-informed-organizational-toolkit.

There are three parts to the Trauma-Informed Organizational Toolkit: a self-assessment, which focuses on evaluating current practices in order to adapt services, programming, and outreach with the goal of becoming a trauma-responsive organization; the user's guide, which offers handholding throughout the self-assessment process; and a how-to manual for creating organizational change, which outlines the essential action steps organizations can pursue on their journey to being trauma-informed and trauma-responsive.

Roger Fallot and Maxine Harris made their Self-Assessment and Planning Protocol for trauma-informed services available in 2006. This document tries to give clear and consistent guidelines for organizations, such as libraries, to modify their service systems in alignment with trauma-informed practices. The assessment has six domains and tackles both services-level and administrative or systems-level changes. Each domain guides the conversation using general and then more specific questions. The document is accessible online at www.theannainstitute.org/TISA+PPROTOCOL.pdf.

Fallot and Harris divide the assessment and planning protocols into six domains that address services-level and administrative-level changes:

1. Program procedures and settings
2. Formal services policy
3. Trauma screening, assessment, and service planning: trauma-specific services
4. Administrative support for program-wide services
5. Staff trauma training and education
6. Human resources practices

These domains include various subdomains. Each of the six domains includes guiding questions for collaborative discussion of an organization's services, physical settings, and so on, along with a list of more specific questions that indicate a trauma-informed approach. In addition, there is a Trauma-Informed

Self-Assessment Scale, which affords library staff the opportunity to assess their current practices and potentially track their progress in aligning with trauma-informed customer services in libraries. The third domain, trauma screening, assessment, and service planning, is oriented toward health service, so it will not be treated here. I will focus on the other five domains, which are the ones most relevant to libraries.

Program Procedures and Settings

The first domain under scrutiny is that of procedures and settings, which include subdomains for the five guiding principles of trauma-informed practice: safety, trustworthiness and transparency, choice, collaboration, and empowerment. First, libraries should identify their key formal and informal activities, services, and settings. List the sequence of service-related activities in which patrons are involved (e.g., outreach, circulation, reference). Identify the library staff who have contact with patrons at each point in this process. Next, identify the settings where library activities take place (e.g., circulation desk, information commons, private offices, other service desks). Then begin with the safety subdomain questions:

1. Where is customer service delivered?
2. When are customer services delivered?
3. Who is present? Are security personnel present? What effect do other patrons, library staff, and security personnel have on service delivery?
4. Are doors locked or open? Are exits easily marked and accessible?
5. How would you describe the service desks? Are they comfortable and inviting?
6. Are restrooms easily accessible?
7. Is the patron's first contact with library staff welcoming, respectful, engaging?
8. Do patrons receive clear explanations and information about each task and procedure? Are rationales explicit? Are specific goals and objectives clear? Does each contact conclude with information sharing the next steps for the library patron?
9. Are library staff attentive to signs of patron distress, discomfort, and unease? Do library staff understand the signs of trauma in an informed manner?
10. What events have occurred in the library that indicate a lack of physical or emotional safety? Events like arguments, conflicts, assaults? What triggered these incidents? What plans are in place to minimize their reoccurrence?
11. Is there adequate personal space for each patron?
12. When making physical contact with patrons, is there sensitivity to potentially unsafe situations (e.g., domestic violence)?

Next are the trust and transparency questions:

1. Does the library provide clear information about what will be done, by whom, when, why, under what circumstances, and at what costs? What are the library's goals when it comes to serving patrons?
2. Where do boundaries veer from the strictly professional? Is there a friendly, relational vibe (e.g., personal information-sharing, touching, exchanging contact information, contact outside of professional settings)? Or do strict professional boundaries exist? Or, is it somewhere in between and dependent on individual behaviors and expressions?
3. How does the library handle overlap in services between library staff?
4. How does the library communicate reasonable expectations to the library staff about customer service delivery?
5. Is the informed consent process relevant for library services?

Third, there are questions about choice and patron control:

1. How much choice do library patrons have over what service they receive? Control over when, where, why, and by whom?
2. Does the library patron choose how contact is made?
3. Does the library build in small choices that make a difference to library patrons? (e.g., "When shall I call? What is the best number for you? What other means of communication do you prefer?")
4. How much control does the patron have over establishing or stopping library services?
5. How are library patrons informed about the choices and options available?
6. How much weight do library patrons' choices have in terms of services received and goals for the effective delivery of those services?
7. How many library services are contingent upon participating in other services? Must the library patron complete a survey in order to receive library instruction, a follow-up phone call, and so on?
8. What messaging exists to inform library patrons about their rights and responsibilities when using library services?
9. Are there negative consequences for making certain choices? Are those necessary, default, or arbitrary consequences?

Fourth, there are questions about collaboration:

1. Do library patrons play a significant role in planning and evaluating the library's services, collections, and programs? How is this role accommodated within the organizational planning? Are members of these advisory groups self-identified as trauma survivors? Do they recognize that their role serves and advocates for other library patrons?
2. Do library staff communicate respect for patrons' experience?
3. Are library patrons' preferences considered or heavily weighted in

planning, goal setting, and the development of library priorities?
4. Are patrons involved as frequently as they should be in library meetings? Are their priorities elicited and validated? Or does their lack of knowledge result in their being steered by the library administration's agenda?
5. Does the library cultivate a model of working with patrons, rather than to or for patrons?
6. Do library staff identify tasks on which they and library patrons can work simultaneously?

Fifth, there are questions about empowerment:
1. Do library patrons who survived trauma have a significant advisory voice in the planning and evaluation of library services?
2. Within the daily service desk workflow, how are library patrons' strengths and skills recognized?
3. Does the library communicate positively and realistically about the ability of library patrons to have their information needs met?
4. Does the library emphasize growth in patron information literacy more than maintenance or stability?
5. Does the library foster the inclusion of library patrons in key roles in planning and evaluation, where possible?
6. How does the library make each patron feel validated and affirmed?
7. How can each interaction between a staffer and a patron focus on skill development or skill enhancement?

Formal Services Policy

Regarding the formal service policies, we should ask how they reflect an understanding of trauma survivors' needs, strengths, and challenges. Libraries need to ensure that their policies regarding confidentiality are clear, that they protect patron privacy, and that their methods are communicated to patrons. Libraries should have clearly written, easily assessable statements of library patrons' rights and grievance channels.

Administrative Support

The next domain tackles administrative support for program-wide trauma-informed services, proposing questions like the following:
1. Is there a policy statement about the importance of accounting for trauma in the delivery of library services?
2. Is there a trauma initiative?
3. Are there workgroups or trauma specialists on hand in the library?
4. Does the library administration work closely with an advisory group of library patrons who are trauma survivors?
5. How willing are administrators to attend trauma training?

6. Are they allocating their own time to trauma-focused work?
7. How well do they retain information about trends in trauma initiatives?
8. Have library administrators made basic resources available in support of trauma-informed service changes and adaptations?
9. Do library administrators support trauma-specific services?
10. Have library administrators found funding to support trauma training and education for library staff?
11. What is the library administration's commitment to the training of library staff?
12. How closely does the library administration monitor trauma-informed service changes?

Staff Training and Education

The next domain deals with trauma training and education for the library staff. The following questions are proposed:
1. Was general education offered to all library staff?
2. Do library staff understand the underlying cause of unusual or difficult library patron behaviors?
3. What training have library staff received regarding maintaining personal and professional boundaries (e.g., confidentiality, dual relationship, sexual harassment)?

Dual relationships sometimes exist because as librarians, people we know already seek us out for help, and we need to be conversant in honoring ethical boundaries and not be confused about the division between personal and professional boundaries. While these boundaries may not be applicable to librarians, they are sometimes relevant within therapy situations.

Human Resources Practices

The last domain examines whether trauma-related concerns are part of the hiring and annual review of staffers' performance in the workplace.
1. Does the library seek out or identify among its current staff "trauma champions," that is, those who know about trauma and its effects?
2. Do prospective staff interviews contain trauma-informed content?
3. Are staffers asked what they know about providing trauma-informed library services?
4. Does the library administration include incentives, bonuses, or promotions for library staff who actively participate in trauma-informed training and practices?
5. Is trauma-informed care part of the onboarding of new workers?

To conclude, undertaking the assessment of organizational readiness is in itself quite a time-consuming task that may take weeks or even months to complete. The data gathered from answering the questions for the various domains (in the numbered lists above) should come from as many sources as possible. In fact, the majority of data should spring from those library staff who work most intimately with patrons. Library administrators can wall themselves off and have zero understanding of daily operations and staff-patron interactions on the granular level, and this is problematic if the only person answering the questions is the one who is least informed or capable of answering them.

12

The Library as Sanctuary

People have always turned to the library for help with their information needs, or merely as a calm and peaceful space. At some point in the second half of the twentieth century, however, American libraries attained a status as safe spaces offering respite to their communities in times of crisis, turmoil, and unrest—both personal and societal. In other words, they became "sanctuaries." For the most part, the literature on this topic has focused on public libraries and school libraries. Academic and special libraries rarely fall into our immediate ideas of sanctuary, though when people envision a library sanctuary, certain well-known academic libraries here and abroad do come to mind.

Sometimes the library is a sanctuary from a toxic school or workplace. K–12 students may escape the competition, bullying, intimidation, harassment, and discrimination they face by visiting the school library. Finding sanctuary in the school library allows youth to escape the social landscape and academic pressures inherent within their experiences. School librarians can offer these students respite and succor for short periods of time, which can help them cope with the pressures of each day. The library also functions as a sanctuary in academia. Students in higher education regularly escape campus housing or residences so that they can find a space—typically the library—where they can focus on their schoolwork, free from distractions like roommates and interruptions from partners and friends. Even faculty members regularly leave their offices and hole up in college and university libraries so they can escape from various unwanted pressures: bullying from other academics, the parents of students asking intrusive questions, students petitioning for higher grades they didn't earn, deans interrupting their research with departmental demands on their time, and so on. In this way, faculty members can focus on their research and scholarship without being inundated by students.

In past decades, Carol Hastings Carpenter (1989) and Michael Cart (1992) explored the library as an area of sanctuary in their respective articles. Carpenter's focus is on high school libraries. She characterizes kids who end up in the high school library as "a few students with underdeveloped or nonexistent social skills and poor peer relations. The others call them nerds or nerdettes or gonzos or bozos. They blush and stumble and mutter and break out." She describes these awkward souls as "mixed race" and "pudgy." With advocates like Carpenter, it's no wonder that some young adults have library anxiety by the time they arrive at college and university libraries! Her descriptions of awkward and socially isolated high school students are pejorative, but in the end, she stresses that "you are there for them," meaning that librarians should be there for these students—but just as an adult presence overseeing the collection and space, not in an empathetic, trauma-informed way. Carpenter's take on the high school library as a sanctuary for awkward souls is as a "haven from the hooligans." Even though Carpenter lacked empathy, she showed a student sympathy by referring him to a teen romance novel in which he drowned his sorrows after a brief love had been found and lost. In the end Carpenter felt rewarded because the student learned from this experience that libraries are warm and safe and that fiction could provide him with respite and comfort, and instruction on the real world. The student also learned the transformative and transportive powers of reading, which allows young people to inhabit characters very different from themselves and try on characteristics they themselves don't have, like bravery or being handsome. Likewise, reading the words of someone who shares the same experiences can help youth feel understood in a way that the people in their real lives have been unable to do. In a nutshell, the library gave this student *sanctuary*.

Cart's examination of the public library begins with his recollection of finding sanctuary in his small hometown public library as a child. He provides a historical context for the term *sanctuary* as being a sacred place of refuge or asylum and discusses churches' role in providing sanctuary for seekers. He describes the similarities between churches and public libraries: they are both places of peace and of celebration. Cart's childhood experiences with public libraries always inspired joy and hope in his life. He recalled the "peaceful, secure quiet of the place. . . ." Like Carpenter, his focus is on the library as a place and space, not on librarians themselves and what actions they can take, or what services they can individually provide. Later on, Cart worked as a page at his public library and encountered the homeless.

Finding sanctuary in his public library as a young adult made Cart pursue professional employment as a librarian. (Anecdotally, this mirrored my own professional path. I sought and found sanctuary in my junior high school library from girls who bullied me in the cafeteria at lunchtime. That same year, I took the bus downtown to my public library after school as one of the "latchkey children" who pursue the calm and community promised by the building and the people working in it. The library was safe, and while I spent time alone there finishing homework or exploring all the questions I had about life, I was surrounded by adults and peers who were a sort of surrogate family.) For his part, Cart eventually became the director of the Beverly Hills (CA) Public Library, where he encountered the "newly deinstitutionalized mentally ill" of the 1970s. Then in the 1980s he dealt with the "second great wave of the homeless." In his article he narrates his experiences with two different homeless women, the first called "Dr. X" and the second called the "Shopping Cart Lady." Cart believed that the real issue was the unresolved one of the library's role as sanctuary.

In 1988 Frances A. Dowd randomly sampled U.S. public libraries and discovered that a majority of respondents said their libraries were being used as day care for unattended children. Likewise, the respondents assumed that parents felt comfortable with their children spending time alone at the library because that space was considered to be "safe." Most public libraries responded to this situation by establishing restrictive policies, while others innovated with creative efforts at serving unaccompanied children. Divorce rates in the United States skyrocketed in the 1970s and 1980s, often resulting in households with a single mother who was unable to supervise her children after school because she was employed. The same problem was occurring with parents who were married but who both held full-time jobs. This problematic situation led to large numbers of "latchkey children," so identified by a house key worn around their neck that allowed them to enter their residence after school. In 1986 a staff writer for the *Los Angeles Times*, Sue Avery, described how more than fifty children turned up at a public library after school.

In his 1992 article, Cart considers the scads of latchkey children hanging out in Los Angeles's public libraries as high-spirited and as potential problems. He contends that librarians are ill-equipped to serve as surrogate parents for these children, nor are they equipped to foster positive self-esteem in them. Instead, Cart calls for child welfare programming from other community organizations, because due to their low staffing and funding, public libraries are unable to serve the needs of latchkey children. In the end, Cart deems the library to be a neutral place of illumination where all are welcome and where we can come together in community, regardless of our race, culture, or ethnic identity. Philosophies have changed since Cart wrote his article in 1992, and it is now recognized that young adult and children's librarians can directly affect the self-esteem and agency of the young people in their communities.

Many people may not consider prison libraries as sanctuaries. However, prison libraries offer inmates an escape from the rigid, highly regulated prison environment. McGee (2019) writes that within the prison library sanctuary, the incarcerated are free to be scholars, academics, or lawyers. Prison libraries offer inmates the opportunity to develop their literacy skills, since research has shown that a majority of prisoners have reading levels below those of ninth graders. Millsap (2018) states that inmates tend to avoid libraries because of their low literacy level and have little understanding of the literacy services that librarians provide to the public. After working with Millsap, inmates confided that they found the prison library a safe space within the prison where the librarian displayed no judgment about their literacy levels or choice of reading materials, and instead encouraged them to continue their forays into reading.

In 2004, Sylvia Leigh Lambert examined the public library as a sanctuary for inner-city youth in her library science master's paper at the University of North Carolina at Chapel Hill. She drew upon ALA's statement that "libraries offer sanctuary. Like synagogues, churches, mosques, and other sacred space, libraries can create a physical reaction, a feeling of peace, respect, humility, and honor that throw the mind wide open and suffuses the body with a near-spiritual pleasure" (*American Libraries* 1995, 1113–19). Lambert's thesis examined the history of the idea of sanctuary all the way from Egyptian, biblical, Greek, Roman, and Anglo-Saxon contexts to the Jeffersonian American one. She also reviewed the United States' identity as a refuge for immigrants from around the globe, and specifically for Jews during and after the Holocaust. She fully explored the notion of sanctuary from both religious and political standpoints and interwove those beliefs with professional librarians' ideals and values. She suggested that librarians' defense of free speech rights established libraries as spaces offering sanctuary for people espousing and expressing all kinds of beliefs. Furthermore, she found evidence of the library as sanctuary in a variety of places, and more specifically from writers who have relied on libraries for research and social assistance, and also, in the case of Columbine High School in 1999, as a place to hide in the midst of a school shooting.

THE SANCTUARY MODEL

Sandra Bloom (2000) led a team of clinicians in a Philadelphia hospital unit in the 1980s from which the Sanctuary Model originated. The model evolved for two decades before human services systems adopted it. The Sanctuary Model is a methodology for changing an organization's culture so that the organization can more effectively heal clients from traumatic psychological and social experiences. The model is designed for training human services workers in trauma-informed care. Bloom described it as "a theory-based, trauma-informed, trauma-responsive, evidence-supported, whole culture approach that has a clear and structured methodology for creating or changing an organizational culture" (2000, 110). Bloom's system for rebooting organizations is specific to group care settings. So while not ideal for customer service operations in libraries, given its human services focus in a clinical setting, there are lessons that library leaders and staff can learn from examining Bloom's model.

Bloom believes that her Sanctuary Model can be applied to any organization. An organization's success in adopting the model depends on collaboration and cooperation between people operating at all levels of the organization. The model's structure and common language bring together practitioners in nursing, social work, psychiatry, and other professions so that they work toward common goals of serving clients in the most thoughtful, informed manner. The more library customer services bleed into social services, the more applicable the Sanctuary Model becomes for our libraries' organizational learning. After training with the model, data revealed that human services organizations see palpable improvement in four areas: (1) morale, (2) a decrease in staff burnout, (3) a decrease in worker's compensation applications and vicarious trauma (trauma transferred from clients to staff), and (4) a decrease in client violence and the need for seclusions and restraint.

Bloom stressed that professionals working with traumatized populations need to be secure, healthy, and possess above-average emotional management skills. Intellectual and emotional intelligence are key as well. Keep in mind that above all, these professionals are tasked with constant emotional labor and must offer or display proficiency in teaching new skills to clients. Given what we learned about ACEs scores, the probability that professionals working in human services experienced traumatic childhoods themselves are high. Self-reflection and acknowledgment of their own unresolved psychological challenges are essential for serving the needs of others. Bloom recognizes that while working with clients creates a certain amount of stress in workers' lives, the main cause of workplace stress is not so much the client as it is the organization's operations.

The Sanctuary Model outlines nine components that are required for creating a trauma-informed organization. First is an organizational mission and value system that support a culture of healing and transformation. Second is having the appropriate workforce or retraining existing workers within a trauma-informed model. Third is shared organizational knowledge and understanding of trauma-based theories and practices as they are embedded within the organization's culture. Fourth is a shared language between administrators, workers, and clients. Fifth is assessment and case formulation (the latter is not applicable to library customer services). Sixth is a process for understanding and managing individual and group dynamics and behavior. Seventh is individualized trauma-informed treatment plans, interventions, and other social services methods (this is not relevant for libraries). Eighth is a method for ensuring that all of the above components are created, incorporated, and integrated into the organization's functioning. Lastly, ninth is making sure that the organizational system works for everyone.

Bloom built the Sanctuary Model via the four pillars of sanctuary: trauma theory, the sanctuary commitments, SELF, and the sanctuary toolkit. The sanctuary commitments are tied to the organization and its function: commitment to nonviolence, commitment to emotional intelligence, commitment to social learning, commitment to open communication, commitment to democracy, commitment to social responsibility, and commitment to growth and change.

Trauma theory is what establishes a baseline for workers providing empathy and service delivery to traumatized populations. Once all workers understand the pervasiveness of toxic stress due to the effects of childhood trauma upon clients and themselves, they can recognize that the behaviors encountered in coworkers, clients, and themselves are not bad or abnormal, but are actually quite typical and normal for those dealing with toxic stress.

SELF stands for Safety, Emotions, Loss, and Future, the four aspects of recovery from traumatic experiences, and is part of the Sanctuary Toolkit. When workers struggle because of stress or secondary trauma, reminding themselves of the SELF compass enacts a cognitive behavioral therapy (CBT) approach to move them through the Sanctuary Model. Clients and workers begin by understanding safety, which includes physical, psychological, social, and moral safety. The meanings and understandings behind these kinds of safety are explained and explored within the organization and the self for deep knowledge. Understanding emotions, their origins, and dealing with them effectively is the second direction in the compass. Acknowledging and coping with the adversity and loss that clients and workers have experienced due to childhood trauma is the third direction. The bridge between this direction and the fourth one asks people to honor their losses but intentionally work toward the future. And focusing on and envisioning a positive future is the fourth direction. These four directions help people who are struggling with trauma's disruption to name and categorize their problems. Bloom said that once a problem is named and categorized, then it can be managed.

Bloom's rationale for the Sanctuary Model is that once an organization's culture is altered, everyone who interacts with the organization is positively affected by those changes. Bloom believes that systematic and systemic intervention is vital for serving the needs of populations that are coping with the effects of childhood trauma. The transformative and residual effects of Bloom's trauma-informed and trauma-responsive Sanctuary Model offer promise for all types of libraries and their models and practices of customer service.

LIBRARY AS PLACES OF SANCTUARY
IN SANCTUARY CITIES

In 2017 President Donald Trump signed two executive orders threatening to cut off federal support to sanctuary cities. Sanctuary cities' laws protect undocumented immigrants from deportation and prosecution. Basically, the cities' municipal laws don't offer up information or local law enforcement resources to assist the federal government's enforcement of immigration rules, laws, and initiatives. For example, San Francisco's sanctuary city ordinances prohibit city employees from using city funds or resources to assist Immigration and Customs Enforcement (ICE) in the enforcement of federal immigration laws unless the assistance is required by federal or state law. Trump alleged that sanctuary cities are "hotbeds of crime." In response to Trump's executive orders, Laura Sanders, an assistant professor at Simmons University, blogged about public libraries' long history of welcoming and serving immigrant populations. She characterized public libraries as the ultimate sanctuary space, citing them as being free to all people, at all times. And she shared how proud she was that libraries in sanctuary cities, like Somerville, Massachusetts, had affirmed their commitment to provide sanctuary spaces to those in need.

However, Sanders failed to mention another reason why libraries as places of sanctuary is a good idea: our professional ethics regarding patrons' rights to privacy. Librarians uphold the First Amendment, which covers free speech, free thought, and free association. Librarians protect patron confidentiality by divorcing identifiable patron information from the circulation or access of items. We do not monitor our patrons' access to information, and in much the same way that sanctuary cities' ordinances operate, libraries do not voluntarily aid and abet law enforcement agencies and officers when they suspect that library records may contain information of use to their investigations of criminal activity. In fact, librarians rebelled against the USA PATRIOT Act, signed into law by President George W. Bush after the terrorist attacks on the World Trade Center and the Pentagon on September 11, 2001. The ALA resolved that the PATRIOT Act endangered citizens' constitutional rights, as well as their rights to privacy. In 2005 the FBI demanded library records from a Connecticut library. The ACLU said the FBI was using an administrative subpoena known as a "national security letter" as a means to procure records related to library patrons, as well as their reading materials, and obtain insight into patrons' use of the Internet. In 2007 a federal judge ruled that two provisions of the act violated the Fourth Amendment because they allowed search warrants to be issued without justifying probable cause.

Public libraries are also sanctuaries in times of civic unrest. Sanders cited the services that the Ferguson (MO) Public Library continued to provide to adults and children during rioting there after the fatal shooting of Michael Brown, and the fact that the Enoch Pratt Free Library stayed open during unrest in Baltimore after the lack of police accountability related to Freddy

Gray's death. In Megan Cottrell's (2015) Q & A with Carla Hayden, Hayden cited the Enoch Pratt Library's role as an anchor for the community as a reason for keeping its branches open, since they serve their communities in both good times and bad times.

Specifically in reaction against to Trump's executive orders, some college campuses declared themselves as sanctuaries. They have adopted policies which refuse cooperation with ICE officials. These colleges stood behind undocumented students because they wanted to ensure their safety in pursuing higher education while also resisting deportation. Academic libraries responded to the Trump administration's executive orders on immigration as well. DePaul University president Dennis H. Holtschnieder reaffirmed the university's commitment to international faculty, staff, and students affected by the order. DePaul faculty and librarians took part in a summit meeting on library services provided to refugees and those seeking asylum. Oberlin University's Sanctuary Project commenced in spring 2017, thus providing context for that school's long history of helping refugees, starting with the Underground Railroad. The City College of San Francisco's library supported its campus and the broader community by creating a resource and research guide on immigration issues, and specifically on sanctuary and immigration policies.

13

Becoming a Trauma-Informed Library Workforce

library workers are helpers, though some may argue that we're not a "traditional" helping profession. The helping professions typically include doctors, nurses, mental health counselors, criminal justice workers, human services professionals, public health workers, and social workers. Laura van Dernoot Lipsky (2018) asserts that people working in the helping professions are routinely exposed to trauma; it comes with the job. In *Simple Self-Care for Therapists* (2015), Ashley Bush Davis likens the secondary trauma that workers in the helping professions absorb daily to inhaling secondhand smoke all day. These workers are not making poor health decisions by smoking cigarettes, but their long-term health is affected by their secondary, casual exposure to trauma displayed by those with whom they interact and serve.

Library workers are also affected by the work that we do. Whether we're directly exposed to traumatic events, or are indirectly feeling the results of natural disasters, terrorist events, or rioting, we experience secondary exposure by hearing our patrons speak out about their traumas, and even by helping them with the resources they need to realign their lives. We help our traumatized patrons when they've recently been victimized or traumatized. Having the emotional wherewithal and the professional and personal resilience to serve our patrons requires consistent and organized plans for self-care.

Sloan, Vanderfluit, and Douglas's article "Not 'Just My Problem to Handle': Emerging Themes on Secondary Trauma and Archivists" (2019) uncovers themes in what constitutes a traumatic record. Traumatic records may document human rights' abuses, controversial material, war, genocide, or more local events like the murder of a family member. It also describes how working with donors and researchers can trigger or re-traumatize archivists, and other areas for concern. They discuss the need for further research into these topics, but clearly, archival education and spaces reorienting themselves as a "caring profession" aligns with the trauma-informed framework's emphasis on self-care and "caring" as a model for customer service.

EMOTIONAL LABOR

While we are not specifically tasked with meeting the emotional and physical needs of our patrons, we do in fact perform emotional labor in communicating with them. Our physical spaces provide comfort, peace, and sanctuary for adults, children, and teens. Although stereotypes about cold, harsh, robotic librarians still persist, modern professional expectations in our libraries require those working with the public to display emotional intelligence and perform emotional labor. Matteson and Miller (2013) stated that library employees must perform emotional labor that requires an awareness of appropriate and professional emotional displays, as well as self-regulation on the employee's part to meet those expectations. They characterize these performances as either "surface" or "deep" acting. Smiling about everything regardless of our real feelings is "surface" acting, but it can still be exhausting.

According to figures from 2018 within an AFL-CIO report (2019), 79 percent of librarians are women. "Service with a smile" takes a greater toll on women, given our culture's new expectations for the emotionally authentic delivery of care and safety to our patrons—as opposed to just pointing to books, articles, and encyclopedias. We must be positive, friendly, engaging, and welcoming, and we must smile and make eye contact. When spending extended time with our patrons, we act as coaches, confidants, and friendly faces. While library work is rewarding, it can also be draining due to our interactions with patrons, coworkers, and administrators. Taking care of the library's "housework"—the relational activity that is required when creating connections between library workers and the people they serve—is exhausting, and this type of housekeeping proportionally burdens women more so than men. It requires emotional intelligence skills to read patrons' emotional states and navigate our interactions with them, as well as to manage our own emotions. Stressful work situations, dwindling resources, and skeleton-crew staffing compound the demands for emotional labor placed upon library workers.

According to Mathieu (2012), "compassion fatigue" is a state of profound emotional and physical exhaustion that helping professionals and caregivers can develop over the course of their career as helpers. "Vicarious traumatization" (VT) is when we work with patrons whose traumatic stories transfer onto us. Many times we may not realize that a transference has happened. It is subtle, gradual, and adds to the amount of daily anxiety and stress that many of us carry home with us at the workday's end. VT isn't just one story, it's the hundreds or thousands of stories we've heard over the course of years, or over our professional careers. Depending on the type of library we work in, the region in which we live, and whether we're in an urban, suburban, or rural environment, we all contend with various levels of trauma transferred from our patrons. At this point, many readers may ask: "Isn't this simply burnout dressed up in a trauma-informed approach?" But burnout doesn't always mean that our view of the world is affected, which is one outcome of VT. Burnout combines low job satisfaction with feeling both powerless and overwhelmed in the workplace. VT, by contrast, changes our view of the world into a scary, negative place.

ROLES BORN OF TRAUMA

The primary traumas that occur in library staffers' personal lives can affect the workplace when they bring those experiences into the organization. Some psychologists indicate that traumatized adults may carry their family role with them into the workplace. According to some authors, the six family roles are: caretaker, rescuer/hero, scapegoat, clown, victim/lost child, and manipulator. Library staff can personify one or more of these roles in the library workplace. They feel safe in the role they played in their family of origin, and they transfer this role to their personal and professional relationships.

The caretaker, who is generally emotionally stable, feels responsible for everyone in the library and takes the blame for situations in which others may be punished or held accountable for their actions. An abiding sense of responsibility pervades these caretakers' work life. They seek approval in the workplace by always being accountable and in charge.

The rescuer/hero insists that nothing is wrong in the library. They want everyone outside of the library to believe that everything is normal and fine there. They lie to themselves and to others by wearing a mask and by creating an atmosphere of smoke and mirrors. Sometimes the hero also displays narcissistic traits.

Scapegoats don't pretend that everything is normal and functional within the library. As someone who does not toe the party line, the scapegoat can have problems with authority figures. They are blamed and punished for what goes wrong and become frequent targets of bullying, mobbing, and other passive-aggressive behaviors. If they are able, they usually choose to leave dysfunctional libraries.

Clowns hide behind humor and use silliness, joking, and bonhomie as a strategy for diffusing dysfunctional library workplaces. Given to impeccable timing, they rescue the day with their presence, thus lightening the mood. They are usually well-liked, and their coworkers rely on their antics, instead of asserting themselves, to diffuse situations brimming with an undercurrent of disaffection.

The victim/lost child is quiet and blends into the woodwork. They are loners, and they don't cause a fuss or rock the boat. They hope that by disappearing people will forget that they work in the library. They never have an opinion and they won't support any side in projects, programs, and so on. They pretend that everything is peachy, and they believe that ignoring people and problems will make them disappear.

The manipulator capitalizes on the workplace's dynamics and effectively plays one person off against another so that the outcomes are in the manipulator's favor. They covertly exercise control while presenting an affable, outgoing façade to their coworkers. Operating from a place of entitlement, they strive to make up for what they missed out on or were denied as children in their family of origin. Manipulators often turn into bullies and are unable to form healthy personal and work relationships.

Library staff may also suffer secondary trauma by hearing about it from their colleagues or patrons. The symptoms of secondary trauma include physical exhaustion, insomnia, and headaches. Immune systems can become depleted. Library staff may try to cope by increasing their use of alcohol and drugs. They call in sick to work. They may express anger and irritability and feel an exaggerated sense of responsibility. They may actively avoid patrons or ask for reassignment to a less public part of the library. Secondary trauma can also impair their ability to make decisions. Their short-term memory can fail, they may seem flaky, or become forgetful and may have trouble forming words. Their ability to provide passable levels of customer service declines, which leads to compromised service for library patrons. With increasing levels of emotional exhaustion brought on by secondary trauma, library workers may distance themselves from patrons and their colleagues. All of these negative effects reduce the library staff's capacity for empathy. Cynicism and embitterment predominate. Once one or more library workers reach these states, the points of customer service begin to fail.

EMPLOYEE EXPERIENCE

Most of us understand the idea behind customer experience (CX) and why that is so very important in attracting and retaining users of our libraries' services, collections, and spaces. CX encompasses users' experiences, emotions, and behavior when using our discovery tools and ILS, our physical spaces and virtual services, and our collections. However, employee experience (EX), according to Denise Lee Yohn (2019), is frequently overlooked. She describes EX as the cumulative exchanges that a worker has with an organization, from recruiting to the exit interview, which can all considerably affect that worker's ability to provide acceptable levels of customer service. Yohn explains that EX is more than just human resources, transparent communication, and organizational social responsibility. She calls for a synthesis between CX and EX and maintains that organizations which prioritize CX over EX sabotage themselves, because in organizations with low EX ratings, the employees tend to perform below par and have higher rates of absenteeism and turnover. In sum, Yohn says that companies fail to realize that an above-average employee experience precedes above-average customer experience. This is certainly true in the library literature. Melilli, Mitola, and Hunsaker (2016), for example, address employee experience in libraries in their research, though this concerns the student employee experience, viewed as a student retention strategy.

Yohn's assertions mirror my own professional experience as someone who has worked in public, medical/special, and academic libraries for over two decades. Instead of examining internal systems for gaps and failures, the majority of administrators with whom I've worked focus more on external issues like funding, staffing, and altering service models as a means for improved function, without grasping that the organization's culture, values, beliefs, and behaviors are causing the dysfunction, and the eventual breakdown of customer service. Organizational self-reflection and learning are the basic and essential building blocks behind both excellent customer experience/service and excellent employee experience.

TOXIC WORKPLACES

Twenge (2017) said that the number of people who feel isolated and left out has reached an all-time high. Holt-Lunstad et al. (2015) write about a "loneliness epidemic" in their study of social connectedness. They credit social isolation and loneliness for increased global morbidity and mortality. All workplaces, but especially libraries, where those external to the space seek sanctuary, can counter this "loneliness epidemic." Some libraries may try to reduce patron isolation by offering robust community events where like-minded people can attend and form valuable connections with each other. Other libraries may be unable to contribute to the community on such a scale, but they can turn inward and examine their own library workplace for evidence of toxicity. Then, by working to eradicate those signs and manifestations and replacing those negatives with positive organizational culture elements, they can neutralize a toxic library workplace and offer smaller but satisfying one-on-one experiences for all.

We feel it, and research supports it: we are exhausted and overwhelmed by our jobs. Whether library administrators explicitly overburden us with too many tasks, or implicitly assume that the library workforce has no work/life balance, the stress we undergo remains the same. Some library workers lack support from the administration for taking earned time off. Library cultures can change dramatically from one administration to the next and slide down to a bad place by putting the wrong person in charge. The overwhelming stress decreases our productivity, effectiveness, and happiness, thus creating low morale (see Kaetrena Davis Kendrick's work on this widespread problem among academic librarians). For those working a traditional Monday-to-Friday workweek, dreading Sundays and the inability to enjoy the whole day off is typical because we anticipate Monday looming on the horizon, which promises just another day at the toxic and stressful workplace.

One strategy for neutralizing toxicity is to approach library meetings differently. Naturally, meetings between library staff and the administration exist along a continuum. Some may be collegial and warm, some may be abrasive and chilly, and some may flip-flop between these extremes over the course of the meeting. General library dysfunction often appears in formal meetings. People talking over each other, having side conversations, or interrupting when people are speaking, are all signs of team dysfunction and disrespect for whoever is speaking. Alternately, no one talking at all is also a sign of team dysfunction and may indicate a fear of sharing ideas with the group because participants have been verbally attacked or have seen it happen to others. Silence may also indicate some participants' complete disengagement from their coworkers, especially if they display negative body language or are allowed to bury their attention in mobile devices or laptops under the guise of following the agenda or note-taking.

The library team needs to collaborate and agree on how its members will work together. An important first step is to create a safe team environment. For example, when a new dean joined my library, the dean discovered that people did not respect each other in meetings and that one person in particular was shouting over everyone, interrupting everyone, and having side conversations that competed for attention and volume with the dean's agenda. In response, the dean instituted a policy whereby people who wanted to speak held up their hand to be acknowledged, so that everyone could be heard in turn. While this helped the team dynamic tremendously, it was also a passive-aggressive strategy the dean used instead of meeting directly with the person who was unprofessional and asking them to change their behavior. This passive-aggressive strategy continued a legacy of silence, secrecy, and workarounds, when dealing with problems directly would have been a more effective response. This type of behavior is common in opaque organizations that have poor communication channels. The same dean drafted guidelines for behavioral expectations in our meetings and posted them without input from any faculty or staff. We were simply told to follow those rules. This top-down approach to making and instituting "rules" diverges from the TIC model. Jerry Colonna (2019) describes this dynamic as one that is underlain by quiet, seething anger. He suggests that conflict avoidance isn't really that but is a response to leftover childhood fears and other old patterns. When conflicts are driven underground, they don't remain buried. They emerge in the form of resentments, frustrations, and other negative feelings that can drive an organization's dysfunction.

ANTIDOTES TO TOXICITY

Spending twenty minutes together at a meeting to outline agreements beforehand, or at least doing so in the future, is valuable for libraries and for any group of people. I learned this practice as part of a workshop I attended in order to become an Our Whole Lives: Lifespan Sexuality Trainer. The idea of outlining agreements for group meetings and behavior was novel to my experience. I mention this practice within this context, in part, to provide examples of how other organizations handle meetings, outside of following Roberts Rules of Order, as well as to illuminate the importance of including everyone in the making of the rules. As you may recall, part of the trauma-informed framework calls for choice and empowerment. When people attending meetings and/or trainings are involved in the operational aspects by coming up with agreements, then they're given choices and are empowered through the process. The training was developed by the Unitarian Universality Association and the United Church of Christ. Our Whole Lives programs are used by faith communities as well as public and private K–12 schools, youth groups, homeschoolers, colleges, and correctional facilities to provide the sexuality education that many children, adolescents, and adults never receive. The programs are secular, but they convey values of self-worth, sexual health, and responsible behavior, as well as justice and inclusivity. Coming to agreement within this type of program setting is essential for everyone to feel safe, especially when people with different beliefs and values come together to learn about and discuss potentially controversial topics like sexuality education. Unfortunately, I failed to capture our agreements and cannot share them as an example. However, another local organization whose meetings I attend hands out the agreements at the beginning of each meeting and reviews them for everyone attending, as I describe below.

My local PFLAG chapter (formerly Parents and Friends of Lesbians and Gays) has eleven agreements (or rules) that govern the participants' conduct at its meetings. I'm sharing these agreements herein as an example of what groups may develop together. Agreements differ between groups because of the nature of their content, as well as the eleven agreements, to which we've given fanciful but descriptive names, which are (1) Vegas, (2) Can't Touch This, (3) One Diva, One Mic, (4) Share the Stage, (5) Banana, (6) Ouch/Oops, (7) Don't Yuck My Yum, (8) "I" of the Tiger, (9) ELMO, (10) Snaps Not Claps, and (11) Sentence Enhancers.

First, the "Vegas" rule: What happens in Vegas, stays in Vegas. This rule is about privacy and confidentiality. Don't refer to PFLAG out in public, since many participants are not out to family, friends, or their workplace. In many states, LGBTQ people can still lose their jobs and housing because of their sexual orientation or identity.

The second rule, "Can't Touch This," refers to asking and receiving consent before touching anyone. Maybe you want to hug someone because they're sad. Ask first. Or maybe you want to tuck in someone's clothing tag. Ask them first. Physical touching can trigger people suffering from trauma.

"One Diva, One Mic" is about letting the person who is talking have the floor. Don't interrupt.

"Share the Stage" means that you need to let others talk when it is their turn. Don't hog the limelight or all the group's attention.

"Banana" means that sometimes we all slip and make a faux pas, and maybe we don't realize it at the time, but when you realize your mistake, you should address this to the group, and apologize.

"Ouch/Oops" is used to call out hurtful language. Sometimes we don't know what words hurt others, and so this is an agreement that allows everyone to make mistakes, have them pointed out, send around apologies, and then move along with the meeting's agenda.

"Don't Yuck My Yum" means don't tell someone that their favorite book, food, or film sucks. It's just not nice. It's unhelpful, and it's only your opinion.

"'I' of the Tiger" reminds us to only speak for ourselves. If we've only ever worked in special libraries, then we shouldn't try to suggest that things particular to special libraries also apply to school libraries.

"ELMO" stands for "Enough, let's move along." It's easy to get off course or get bogged down during a meeting. We need to respect everyone's time and not get mired in minutiae that should be addressed by a smaller working group, or not addressed at all. Using ELMO acknowledges someone's voice but doesn't allow them to hijack the meeting and hold everyone hostage. It also helps keep people engaged, because once the meeting hijacker gets started, people tend to drift off and stop paying attention. The trick with using ELMO is to introduce this concept at the start of the meeting, and then if someone wanders too far afield, restoring the meeting's agenda is easier. Most of us want efficient meetings that don't waste out time. How many days (or weeks) of your professional life have been spent listening to the library's "historian" who pontificates about how the library worked twenty years ago?

"Snaps Not Claps" removes clapping from the group's dynamic. When people applaud, it easily arrests the meeting's momentum. The noise also makes it difficult to hear when people are trying to get everyone back on track. Moreover, many traumatized people and neurodivergent people are hypersensitive to noise and sound. Protecting everyone from overstimulation is key in meetings. Also, the Snaps Not Claps model returns us to mid-twentieth-century beatnik culture, when coffee shop poets were regaled with snapping fingers, not claps.

Finally, a word about the last rule, "Sentence Enhancers." For most libraries, this one shouldn't even be included in your list of agreements. Sentence enhancers are curse words. Some people like them and use them. Other people hate them and find them triggering. At the start of every local PFLAG meeting, the facilitators take an anonymous poll of attendees about whether curse words are okay with everyone. If they are not, sentence enhancers are prohibited from that meeting.

Having group members develop these agreements (or others) invests them in enforcing agreements and reminding coworkers when they fail to adhere to them. Spreading governance to everyone removes the responsibility for enforcement from the meeting convener. It also allows library workers' input into any group dynamics that they find triggering or re-traumatizing, and thus permits everyone empowerment, voice, and choice in a space where their attendance is required.

SELF-CARE

Self-care allows us to level up our compassion and empathy. Working with patrons, coworkers, the bureaucracy, and administrators can deplete our emotional reserves. Forgoing self-care, or being unaware of its importance, are poor strategies for long-term mental and physical health. When you feel like you kill a small part of yourself every day you show up at work, that is a major problem. The anxiety can range from occasional feelings of being out of your element to months or years of just barely keeping your head above water, after being thrown into a sink-or-swim environment. That's why self-care and peer support are essential elements of the trauma-informed library. Being overwhelmed by situations, personalities, or interactions in the library workplace can be overcome with several personal self-care approaches.

In her book *Simple Self-Care for Therapists* (2015), Ashley Davis Bush introduces the concept of "macro" and "micro" self-care. Macro includes vacations, massages, hobbies, a healthy diet, and exercise; all of these are traditional activities that are essential for self-care. But Bush also suggests "micro" practices that one can summon in the moments between and during normal activities. She categorizes these micro moments of possibility as "calm, awareness, rejuvenation, and balance." Many of us may be familiar with this approach through recent books on reflection and mindfulness in library practice, such as Michelle Reale's *Becoming a Reflective Librarian and Teacher: Strategies for Mindful Academic Practice* (2017) and Richard Moniz et al.'s *The Mindful Librarian: Connecting the Practice of Mindfulness to Librarianship* (2015).

Vivian Brown (2018) suggests developing daily self-care habits as part of a complete program of self-care that includes both macro and micro habits. Micro habits help librarians ground themselves when they're feeling scattered, become energized when they're feeling depleted, and become relaxed when they're feeling bodily manifestations of stress and anxiety such as headaches, muscle tightness, nervous stomach (including diarrhea, constipation and nausea), chest pain and rapid heartbeat, clenched jaw, and so on. These symptoms vary from person to person, since we all handle stress differently.

Just as bodies experience and exhibit stress differently, what works for one person's self-care may be anathema to another. Getting enough quality sleep, regular exercise, and following a nutritionally sound diet are the big three macro areas of self-care that everyone should focus on. Healthy relationships, rewarding hobbies, community involvement, and spiritual connection round out the macro practices. But for some of us, hobbies, massages, and mini vacations are difficult or impossible because of our professional lives and personal obligations. Finding the time, money, and sometimes even the energy for those indulgences can be challenging. This is why incorporating micro practices into our daily routine is essential for our optimal functioning as human beings, and as helpful library workers.

James Clear writes about habit formation in *Atomic Habits: An Easy & Proven Way to Build Good Habits & Break Bad Ones* (2018). His personal experience is that tiny changes can have long-term effects. He suggests creating systems that allow you to succeed at adopting new habits. Beginning small with "I can meditate for one minute," and then gradually increasing the time spent meditating creates a "meditate system." Another suggestion Clear makes is to change your beliefs about yourself. Ask, "Who is the type of person who practices self-care?" It is someone who is self-compassionate and makes time for herself. Throughout the day, ask yourself if your behavior reflects the new identity you're cultivating as a person dedicated to self-care. Clear suggests creating a plan of action with a specific time and place, to help you succeed in developing a good habit. Examples are: "After I arrive in the parking lot at work each day, I will spend the time it takes me to enter the library in walking meditation." Or, "When I leave the library at the end of my day, I will spend the time walking to my car in walking meditation." Once you've practiced this habit enough times, it becomes automatic. Your practice doesn't need to be perfect, either. Clear said that your physical location connects the habits of body and mind.

Ashley Davis Bush recommends micro practices for a variety of times and places. Her list includes practices to use upon waking; for starting your workday; for starting a session, to use in session, or after sessions; and to end your workday. Remember, these practices are actually meant for therapists, who usually have time in-between each session with a client to practice these "moments" and incorporate them into their routine. For library workers, however, adding micro self-care moments in-between editing metadata, or handling reference or circulation transactions, can be tricky. Besides the times that Bush suggested, she makes plain that balancing your micro care moments between breath, movement, mindfulness, and visualization practices, on the one hand, and grounding, energizing, and relaxation practices on the other is essential for optimal human functioning. This seems like a lot to balance to create time for, but you can start small, with just one practice, and once you've made that a habit, add another practice. This is a strategy that Clear advocates as well, and which he calls "habit stacking." Once you've integrated a habitual grounding exercise, add an energizing exercise to your practice.

To be honest, browsing through the exercises that Bush explains in *Simple Self-Care for Therapists* made me quickly dismiss them. They need much adaptation to the library setting and the various service models we function in. Her micro practices don't seem like anything I'm likely to add to my day. I rarely work a public service desk but meet regularly with students one-on-one for research consultation and for formal library instruction sessions. Bush's practices seem like elaborate visualizations divorced from my professional reality (especially the grounding practice "Hark How the Bells," in which one rings a Tibetan singing bowl three times with a client/patron). However, her "Go in Peace" parting ritual seems feasible. Once you conclude your interaction with a library patron, silently offer them equanimity and goodwill as they leave the space. Bush says that this practice clears one's emotional space and helps one transition to the next patron.

The kind of micro self-care practices that you can perform habitually depend a great deal on the type of services you're providing. Those who are working busy service desks and offering constant answers, referrals, and directions to patrons have less room for rituals and formal breaks in-between these activities. But those offering in-depth research consultation or library instruction do have moments in which they can add grounding, energizing, or relaxation practices. Whether we take prescribed breaks or work through them, most employers mandate two fifteen-minute breaks and an hour-long lunch break during the typical eight-hour workday. We make time for what we deem important, and we library workers *are* important.

PLAN FOR SELF-CARE

Developing a self-care plan is an individual project, but the library administration can play a role in encouraging these practices. The administration should generate an awareness of self-care and its importance in the organization. Having outside experts address the library workforce is another approach for creating an organization that recognizes and values self-care. Helping workers devise self-care plans in a workshop or a professional development setting demonstrates the library's commitment to caring for its workforce's welfare. Building in opportunities and providing spaces for self-care within the workday helps workers help themselves.

An authentic commitment to library worker self-care could include the administration scheduling and paying for monthly or quarterly visits to the library by a licensed massage therapist to provide 15–20-minute mini-massages. This would demonstrate the administration's commitment to self-care. Another option is collaborating with local massage schools, since the students of these schools need captive bodies on which to practice and learn. Reminding library workers to take mandated breaks and step away from their desks is a simpler but effective measure libraries can take. Asking library staff to schedule time with themselves for self-care on their calendars makes the practice part of the daily routine. Outfitting break rooms with quiet spaces where people can collect their thoughts while breathing deeply is another suggestion. If break rooms are too small or are heavily trafficked, the administration can set aside other spaces, for example, tech-free or contemplative spaces, where staffers can take a minute and collect themselves. Often, briefly escaping the building completely is helpful for resetting one's attention, and then returning with a renewed focus on empathetic and helpful customer service.

The self-care practices I use while at work include simple actions like taking a break from my tasks and leaving the building for a change of scenery and the opportunity to breathe fresh air and sample the weather. Often I am so occupied that the only breaks I take are to the bathroom. I skip lunch, or cobble together a poor facsimile from vending machines. I added plants to my office space for the health benefits they provide by purifying the air, dampening noises, and for their aesthetics. Fortunately, given my private office, I can use an aromatherapy essential oil diffuser. I limit the amount of artificial, fluorescent lighting in my workspace by keeping the overhead lights turned off. As luck would have it, an exterior window at one end of my office provides an adequate amount of natural light.

When I suspect the day will be tense, I drop peppermint into the diffuser and let it infuse the air in my office. I tend to feel, and store, anxiety and stress in my neck and shoulders, which eventually leads to daily headaches and migraines. Remaining well-hydrated by drinking lots of water each day is suggested for reducing headaches. Seeking relief with a massage therapist twice a month and making changes to my diet has helped reduce the number and severity of the headaches I experience—some of which affect my ability to work at the library that day. Peppermint is commonly used to treat headaches or migraines because the menthol in it helps relax muscles and ease pain. Applying diluted peppermint to the temples can help staunch pain from tension headaches and migraines. I can't vouch for its effectiveness, though; it may be psychosomatic. I also keep a lacrosse ball and a foam roller in my office so that when my shoulders and neck tighten, I can counteract how my body stores anxiety by massaging and loosening the muscles myself, either by lying on the floor on the foam roller or rolling the lacrosse ball between the affected areas of my body and a stationary door or wall. A colleague of mine gets through their day with a series of rituals, including tuning into YouTube videos featuring Tibetan bowls and Japanese Buddhist bells, always leaving the library for lunchtime, regular hot tea infusions, and walks around the library to interact with coworkers.

Once you've left the workplace for the day, opportunities for self-care abound. But first, disconnect from your cell phone. Separate yourself from the library and from all work distractions or communications that may arrive in your device's in-box after you've left work for the day. Limiting e-mail to the middle of the day erects a nice buffer for library staff so that they aren't looking at messages first thing in the morning and right before bedtime. Having this boundary, and building others that separate work time from lifetime, is critical for establishing a consistent self-care practice. Go to the gym. Go outside to a park, forest, gardens, or nature preserve. The Japanese practice forest bathing, or *shinrin-yoku*, which is connecting with nature through all of your senses. Studies indicate that *shinrin-yoku* reduces pulse rates and also decreases scores for depression, fatigues, anxiety, and confusion in middle-aged male subjects. Its benefits may vary if you fall outside of that identity, however.

Limit your use of social media. While connecting with family and friends can be rewarding, social media may leave you feeling less than others if your life lacks material luxuries or other signs of success. Pressure to present only positive, happy images and ideas creates its own brand of stress and anxiety and takes one out of integrity with self. Access nature; your health will improve from fresh air, natural noises, and moving around more. Attend to your sleep hygiene—the main emphasis here is reducing your exposure to blue light a few hours prior to bedtime. Artificial lighting and electronics emit blue light. In humans, exposure to blue light limits melatonin production and alters our circadian rhythms, both of which are necessary for sound sleep.

Don't be afraid to ask for help with your workload in the library and at home. Being independent and self-sufficient, and taking care of all aspects of our work life and our personal life are expected from us as adults. But many of us, either due to our family's values or from absorbing the philosophy and practice of American individualism that Herbert Hoover wrote about, feel that we cannot ask for help. Hoover wrote that individualism is the key to progress and that our pioneer spirit has underpinned America's political, economic, and spiritual institutions for the last three centuries. Our spirit of American individualism has imbued us with the values of stoicism, initiative, and opportunity. But this emphasis on the individual can sometimes preclude our taking comfort from others and asking others for help when we need it. Asking for help makes us seem weak, ineffective, and unable to tend to our duties. Amanda Palmer's TED Talk "The Art of Asking," and her follow-up book *The*

Art of Asking, or How I Learned to Stop Worrying and Let People Help (2014) created a conversation about our cultural reluctance to ask others for help. However, Palmer is indifferent to the fact that racial and class structures discourage many people from asking for what they want and need. Regardless, relying on help from others and asking our colleagues, friends, and family members for help when we need it is one of the most effective forms of self-care available to just about everyone.

Since people might not ask for help when they need it, one of my daily practices is to check in with my immediate colleagues and those whom I supervise. During the check-in I ask how they are, how their work is going, and I listen carefully, observe them with care, and note any concerns. When they're having off days, when they're stressed, or when something may prevent them from being their best at the library that day, I offer my help. If I can relieve a burden so that they feel less stressed, that creates a culture of caring and support within my immediate domain. Last year a colleague asked me to complete a task that she had zero time for completing that week. I finished it in an hour, and my colleague's sense of relief was immense now that the burden had been lifted from her shoulders. Helping her remove that obstacle from her workflow increased my usefulness to her as a colleague, and as a friend. It reduced her stress and frustration at having a staggering workload, and it affirmed our relationship as warm colleagues.

Establishing and sustaining a daily practice of self-care is key to managing the troubling aspects of our day, and shaking off the pressures felt from information overload, clashing personalities, and recurring crises. When everyone is maxed out, we can't contain the stress any longer and it seeps out, sometimes in slow innocuous ways, and other times in hurtful, destructive ways. This creates a feedback loop in which an organization cycles through everyone's stress in a never-ending manner.

Critics of the self-care movement, like Miri Mogilevsky (2017), suggest that the recent emphasis on self-care and burnout by companies is merely a way for exploitative employers to persistently extract high productivity from workers. She contends that companies aren't being held accountable for having created and sustained the dehumanizing and intolerable conditions in the workplace in the first place. Many corporations suggest that workers individually develop thicker skins and strengthen their coping skills, rather than taking responsibility for toxic stress in the workplace and reducing or eradicating it. When library staff are paid low wages and given very little sick and vacation time, a weekly bubble bath can never dent the weariness of the chronically exhausted. Mogilevsky says organizations that look at self-care as an individual rather than a collective responsibility use it as a distraction from the care they fail to give to their employees.

14

Planning for Trauma-Informed Services

After conducting a library's organizational readiness assessment and determining that the library is ripe for change and is committed to trauma-informed organizational change, long-term planning enters the equation. A long-term commitment to establishing trauma-informed customer services in libraries should take a minimum of three years' time.

YEAR ONE

The organization's commitment to trauma-informed care is cemented and assured. The library administration's strategic planning is informed by trauma-informed principles. Organizational documents such as the vision, mission, and value statements are reviewed and updated using language that is recognized as trauma informed. These documents are fluid and evolving and should be updated regularly. Depending on the number of personnel employed by the library, one or two key library staff should be asked to serve as the library's "trauma champions"; that is, those who have some authority to initiate and implement changes and who will be responsible for coordinating the changes and keeping the momentum going. Forming an oversight committee is advisable so that the library's movement toward trauma-informed customer services is clearly plotted. This committee should be a mix of stakeholders: from trustees to community members, to trauma survivors. The self-assessment is conducted within this first year, and an implementation plan is developed. Policy development focused on preventing re-traumatization is a key element in this implementation plan.

Another component of this planning is that of developing or reviewing the library's disaster plan. While the requirements for this vary according to what type of population a library serves, each plan should look at ways to reduce re-traumatization in case of a natural or man-made disaster. Reducing the effects these experiences have upon library patrons is integral to functioning as a trauma-informed library. In library school, over two decades ago, I wrote a paper on disaster preparations and planning in my library management and administration course. Back then, the literature focused on natural disasters like flooding, earthquakes, and fires. Nowadays our profession deals with many more types of disasters and trauma, given the violence pervading our lives since the 9/11 attacks, school shootings, and other events.

Several steps occur in disaster planning. First, assembling a disaster response team and having them properly trained is key. Developing a means of communication during and after the disaster is also necessary. Outlining steps for informing the community about our ability to maintain our services ensures some continuity of service to our patrons. Libraries should develop a method for maintaining the confidentiality of patron records during disasters. Establishing networks with other agencies ahead of time can help library staff give accurate, credible information about other organizations that trauma survivors may be served by. Planning should include prioritizing which library services will be offered, and where, and for what length of time, once the disaster is mitigated. Making accommodations and allowing some leeway for library staff to go above and beyond in providing customer services to trauma survivors during and after disastrous events, under the category of "special services," is advised. Finally, it is essential to convene the library staff a short time after operations have returned to normal functioning, so that everyone can debrief and share information that may improve the effectiveness or efficiency of services when planning for the next disaster.

The last few standards that the library administration and the oversight committee should consider are applying culturally responsive principles in a trauma-informed organization, using science-based knowledge for decision-making and planning, and creating a peer-support environment for library workers and library patrons. Additionally, receiving ongoing feedback and evaluation from library patrons allows the oversight committee to monitor how well the library is meeting its objectives.

Developing a strategic plan for the first year includes identifying and agreeing upon goals. Then the specific steps the library plans to take to reach

each goal must be outlined. Next, the plan identifies and delineates the resources needed for meeting the goals. Finally, it sets up a time frame for achieving each of the goals, and it assigns a person or team responsibility for examining the progress and for documenting the effects this has upon customer service.

For example, if a library determines that customer service at the reference/information desk lacks warmth, the goal is to infuse warmth in the reference relationship. Defining what "warmth" looks and feels like, as well as figuring out how to measure it, are necessary. Training the reference staff in ways to express warmth is key. Offering professional development training around warmth creation is a necessary step. Then conducting that training with the library staff follows. The next step is adding a warmth component to the staff's annual evaluations, so that it is measurable and the staff know how to infuse their reference relationships with that quality. Warmth may, in fact, be so evanescent that defining and measuring it is abandoned for a more objective goal. Adding follow-up or customer service evaluation at the point of service is essential for measuring whether the library patrons experienced warmth. Some questions libraries may use to measure warmth are: "I felt the librarian paid attention to me," "I felt the librarian was empathetic," "I trusted the librarian."

Within the first year an action plan develops. This plan is informed by goal setting around the specific challenges, strengths, and areas identified in the library's self-assessment. One way to approach this is having the library staff generate a list of topics that would help them provide trauma-informed customer services. The staff can then determine if they want to work in small groups, large groups, or otherwise to address the topics and develop policy changes. Outside experts can also address and educate on these topics in library staff meetings.

Setting up a timeline is valuable for measuring success. Dividing it into quarters may be helpful: training in the first quarter, implementation in the second quarter, and then measurement and assessment in the third and fourth quarters, when those responsible for improving the reference desk's warmth factor report on their success, or change the aforementioned warmth goal to something that can be measured and assessed more easily.

Several goals of this type should exist in the year one plan. Focusing on one goal per area is a modest and conservative suggestion for managing this type of customer service change. Besides warmth generation, other areas for improvement may be transparency and patron choice.

YEAR TWO

In the second year, the action plan is implemented and is functioning as envisioned. The action plan serves as a map for organizational change and identifies specific steps needed for becoming a trauma-informed library. Part of the action plan involves the administration creating and communicating the library's future expectations for customer service. The plan outlines the objectives identified earlier where customer service needs strengthening. For the best outcomes, items in the action plan should be very specific. When the vision is too lofty, library workers will be working toward an ephemeral goal without any guidelines for understanding their target. Being mindful of the numbers set as a measure of success is also important. Aiming too high may be a stumbling block and may be distinctly unrealistic. The objectives that are set must work in concert with each other. Library staff should understand how these elements support and build upon each other, otherwise the action plan may seem like a crazy patchwork that lacks cohesion.

Daily, weekly, or quarterly nudges, if appropriate, from supervisors to their library staff can reinforce the trauma-informed vision and goals. Another area of sensitivity includes ensuring that library workers' cognitive load is appropriate during the transition. Asking library staff to add on more—more steps, more behaviors, and more thought—can be too much. Asking for more from library workers before they are ready and willing to adopt this model can also be too much. It leads to low morale and discouragement about the library's mission, vision, and values. Involving library staff in deciding what they will stop doing while they work toward trauma-informed and trauma-responsive changes is crucial in obtaining their buy-in and authentic engagement.

YEAR THREE

Year three includes coaching, refinement of the action plan, assessing what is working and what isn't working, and the review of hard data. Other tweaks can be easily made during year three because the system should be fairly functional by this time; most components for successful trauma-informed operations have matured—or else they have withered and can be discounted as failures. But learning from those failures is key in this process.

Coaching can occur between a variety of individuals and at various levels. For instance, when library staff consistently struggle with a component of customer service they cannot manage, someone with the requisite skill can coach and monitor them until they attain the levels of success expected by the library administration. The old stereotypes about introverted librarians do, after all, have at least some basis in reality. We recognize that some library personalities are better suited to work behind the scenes, while others thrive when working with library patrons. Given staffing shortages, library staff working in the back office may be expected to staff service desks sometimes. And perhaps these staffers consistently lack warmth and come off as robotic. Of course, this too is a stereotype in our libraries: public services vs. technical services. In any case, this situation presents an opportunity for coaching, and specifically "warmth coaching." A modicum of warmth can be learned, or even faked, though the latter is something that trauma survivors can easily sniff out. Even neurodivergent library staff can learn these skills and meet performance standards in this domain. Eye contact, nodding, and smiling are the three key signs of warmth. As long as library workers perform these three things, they can fake warmth. The adage "Fake it until you make it" may also be relevant here. Composing an active listening face, rather than a negatively perceived "librarian's face," is another skill that can be successfully coached.

Polishing the action plan includes reviewing the actions the library said it would take, looking for evidence that the library took those actions, and then investigating how successful the actions proved within the time frame. Careful documentation is necessary for this step's effectiveness. Enhancements may include expanding or constricting the actions, devising methods for measuring the actions' success, and then determining what a measure means.

For instance: what does success look like? Does success value quantity over quality, or vice versa? Does it mean there are zero turnaways (i.e., titles a library does not carry)? Does it mean that applications for library cards have increased by 40 percent? Or that broken links in the library's ILS have been reduced by 20 percent? These are discrete measures by which the library can measure its success. Refining the action plan may mean creating very different measures from what were established in the first year. Using data and making changes based upon that evidence is sound and practical.

A library's relationship with data is important for several reasons. Most libraries count various things and call this "assessment," but this is not assessment, it's just counting. For decades libraries have counted the number of items circulated, the gate count, the number of links clicked, the number of patrons attending programs, the number of reference transactions, and so on. When we gather this sort of information from year to year, we can see incremental changes, and a trend that may show growth or decline. But our focus on numbers, on quantities, and on quantitative data only tells part of the library's story.

In the early 2000s libraries were still focused on counting, though some libraries did administer customer satisfaction surveys to assess their own performance. More recently, however, many libraries have realized that they must demonstrate their value, and especially how their services tie into the goals and strategic planning of their parent organizations. As a result, there is a growing interest in capturing authentic data and in using new methods to not only count numbers, but combine those numbers for a holistic overview in which we can map patterns and derive real meaning from the intersections of those numbers with other data we've gathered anecdotally or from collaborations with other libraries and librarians.

Beyond the third year, libraries should reassess annually by surveying their staff and library patrons, convening focus groups, and performing qualitative interviews with everyone. Likewise, yearly training of staff to keep their skills viable is necessary, as is including trauma-informed training in onboarding efforts when new library staff are hired. Connecting with agencies in the community that have a similar commitment to trauma-informed approaches to customer service can help create a community of care in your locality. Offering training and professional development on an interagency basis can also help cement the TIC network. Outside agencies can help with ongoing training. They can also provide support and consultation if the library encounters unusual behaviors that leave the library staff wondering if there are better means of handling these situations.

Appendix
Adverse Childhood Experience Questionnaire

FINDING YOUR ACE SCORE

While you were growing up, during your first 18 years of life:

1. Did a parent or other adult in the household *often* . . .

    Swear at you, insult you, put you down, or humiliate you?
    or
    Act in a way that made you afraid that you might be physically hurt?

    Yes   No   If yes, enter the number "1" here: _____

2. Did a parent or other adult in the household *often* . . .

    Push, grab, slap, or throw something at you?
    or
    Ever hit you so hard that you had marks or were injured?

    Yes   No   If yes, enter the number "1" here: _____

3. Did an adult or person at least 5 years older than you *ever* . . .

    Touch or fondle you or have you touch their body in a sexual way?
    or
    Try to or actually have oral, anal, or vaginal sex with you?

    Yes   No   If yes, enter the number "1" here: _____

Source: ACES Too High, "Got Your Ace Score?," https://acestoohigh.com/got-your-ace-score/.

4. Did you *often* feel that . . .

> No one in your family loved you or thought you were important or special?
> *or*
> Your family didn't look out for each other, feel close to each other, or support each other?

> Yes   No   If yes, enter the number "1" here: _____

5. Did you *often* feel that . . .

> You didn't have enough to eat, had to wear dirty clothes, and had no one to protect you?
> *or*
> Your parents were too drunk or high to take care of you or take you to the doctor if you needed it?

> Yes   No   If yes, enter the number "1" here: _____

6. Were your parents *ever* separated or divorced?

> Yes   No   If yes, enter the number "1" here: _____

7. Was your mother or stepmother . . .

> *Often* pushed, grabbed, slapped, or had something thrown at her?
> *or*
> Sometimes or often kicked, bitten, hit with a fist, or hit with something hard?
> *or*
> *Ever* repeatedly hit, or threatened with a gun or knife?

> Yes   No   If yes, enter the number "1" here: _____

8. Did you live with anyone who was a problem drinker or alcoholic or who used street drugs?

> Yes   No   If yes, enter the number "1" here: _____

9. Was a household member depressed or mentally ill, or did a household member attempt suicide?

      Yes   No   If yes, enter the number "1" here: _____

10. Did a household member ever go to prison?

      Yes   No   If yes, enter the number "1" here: _____

Now add up your "Yes" answers: _____.
This is your ACE Score.

Once you know your ACE score, what can you do with it? Tallying your ACE score is all about understanding if childhood experiences may have impacted your life. It's also about building empathy for others and understanding that a majority of people have these scores. There are many situations and events that children experience as traumatic that are not accounted for in the test. Therefore, this simple assessment may not reveal the whole picture. Another thing to keep in mind is that we are all different, and every child's experience is unique. Just because a person may score a four or seven or nine does not doom a person to particular mental or physical health outcomes. Children are resilient. This means that they can process and overcome hardship and flourish as adults. The number one predictor of childhood resilience is a stable, responsive relationship with at least one adult. Do keep in mind, however, that some children are more sensitive to environmental factors than others.

References

AFL-CIO, Department for Professional Employees. 2019. "Library Professionals: Facts & Figures." https://dpeaflcio.org/programs-publications/issue-fact-sheets/library-workers-facts-figures/.

Alabi, J. 2015. "Racial Microaggressions in Academic Libraries: Results of a Survey of Minority and Non-Minority Librarians." *Journal of Academic Librarianship* 41, no. 1: 47–53. https://doi.org/10.1016/j.acalib.2014.10.008.

American Libraries. 1995. "12 Ways Libraries Are Good for the Country." December 26, 1113–19.

American Library Association. 1995. "Code of Ethics." www.ala.org/united/sites/ala.org.united/files/content/trustees/orgtools/policies/ALA-code-of-ethics.pdf.

———. 1996. "Library Bill of Rights." www.ala.org/advocacy/intfreedom/librarybill.

———. 2014. "Privacy | Advocacy, Legislation & Issues." www.ala.org/advocacy/intfreedom/librarybill/interpretations/privacy.

———. 2019. "ALA Resolution for the Adoption of Sustainability as a Core Value of Librarianship." www.ala.org/aboutala/sites/ala.org.aboutala/files/content/governance/council/council_documents/2019_ms_council_docs/ALA%20CD%2037%20RESOLUTION%20FOR%20THE%20ADOPTION%20OF%20SUSTAINABILITY%20AS%20A%20CORE%20VALUE%20OF%20LIBRARIANSHIP_Final1182019.pdf.

———. 2010. "Services and Responsibilities of Libraries (Old Number 52)." www.ala.org/aboutala/governance/policymanual/updatedpolicymanual/section2/52libsvcsandrespon#B.8.10.

———. n.d. "USA PATRIOT Act | Advocacy, Legislation and Issues." www.ala.org/advocacy/advleg/federallegislation/theusapatriotact.

Anderson, A. 2018. "Autism and the Academic Library: A Study of Online Communication." *College & Research Libraries* 79, no. 5: 645–58.

Andrews, N. 2018. "Reflections on Resistance, Decolonization, and the Historical Trauma of Libraries and Academia." In *The Politics of Theory and Practices of Critical Librarianship*, ed. M. Seale and K. Nicholson. Sacramento, CA: Litwin Books. https://doi.org/10.31229/osf.io/mva35.

Anglin, D., and C. Sachs. 2003. "Preventative Care in the Emergency Department: Screening for Domestic Violence in the Emergency Department." *Academy of Emergency Medicine* 10, no. 10: 1118–27.

Association of College and Research Libraries. 2012. "Diversity Standards: Cultural Competency for Academic Libraries." www.ala.org/acrl/standards/diversity.

Avery, S. 1986. "Libraries Cope with Latchkey Children." *Los Angeles Times*.

Bath, H. 2008. "The Three Pillars of Trauma-Informed Care." *Reclaiming Children and Youth* 17, no. 3: 17–21. https://eric.ed.gov/?id=EJ869920.

Beard, G. Miller. 1880. *A Practical Treatise on Nervous Exhaustion (Neurasthenia)*. 2nd rev. ed. New York: W. Wood.

Berila, B. 2011. "Queer Masculinities in Higher Education." In *Masculinities in Higher Education: Theoretical and Practical Considerations,* ed. J. A. Laker and T. Davis, 97–111. United Kingdom: Taylor & Francis Group.

Bloom, S. L. 2000. "The Sanctuary Model: Rebooting the Organizational Operating System in Group Care Settings." In *Treatment of Child Abuse: Common Ground for Mental Health, Medical, and Legal Practitioners,* 2nd ed., 109–17. Baltimore, MD: Johns Hopkins University Press.

Brewer-Smith, K., R. T. Pohlig, and G. Bucurescu. 2016. "Female Children with Incarcerated Adult Family Members at Risk for Lifelong Neurological Decline." *Health Care Women International* 37, no. 7: 803–13.

Brown, B. 2010. *Gifts of Imperfection: Let Go of Who You Think You're Supposed to Be and Embrace Who You Are*. Center City, MN: Hazelden Publishing.

———. 2013. "Brené Brown on Empathy." www.youtube.com/watch?v=1Evwgu369Jw.

Brown, V. B. 2018. *Through a Trauma Lens: Transforming Health and Behavioral Health Systems*. New York: Routledge.

Burstow, B. 2003. "Toward a Radical Understanding of Trauma and Trauma Work." *Violence Against Women* 9, no. 11: 1293–1317. https://doi.org/10.1177/1077801203255555.

Bush, A. D. 2015. *Simple Self-Care for Therapists: Restorative Practices to Weave through Your Workday*. New York: W. W. Norton.

Campbell, B. 2018. "Trial Date Set in Gorilla Mask Intimidation Case, More Videos Surfaced." *Johnson City Press*, November 8.

Carpenter, C. H. 1989. "The Library as Sanctuary." *VOYA* 12, no. 8: 146.

Cart, M. 1992. "Here There Be Sanctuary: The Public Library as Refuge and Retreat." *Public Library Quarterly* 12, no. 4: 5–23.

Centers for Disease Control and Prevention. 2012. "Child Abuse and Neglect Cost the United States $124 Billion." www.cdc.gov/media/releases/2012/p0201_child_abuse.html.

———. n.d. "Adverse Childhood Experiences." www.cdc.gov/violenceprevention/childabuseandneglect/acestudy.

Cerulo, E., and C. Mazur. 2019. *Work Wife: The Power of Female Friendship to Drive Successful Business*. New York: Random House.

Chodron, P. 2019. *Welcoming the Unwelcome: Wholehearted Living in a Brokenhearted World*. New York: Penguin Random House.

Clear, J. 2018. *Atomic Habits: An Easy & Proven Way to Build Good Habits & Break Bad Ones*. Garden City, NY: Avery Publishing Group.

Colonna, Jerry. 2019. *Reboot: Leadership and the Art of Growing Up*. New York: Harper Business.

Cottrell, M. 2015. "Baltimore's Library Stays Open During Unrest." *American Libraries*. americanlibrariesmagazine.org/blogs/the-scoop/qa-carla-hayden-baltimore/.

Covington, S. 2018. *Moving from Trauma-Informed to Trauma-Responsive: A Training Program for Organizational Change*. Center City, MN: Hazelden Publishing.

Day, Daniel. 2019. *Dapper Dan: Made in Harlem: A Memoir*. New York: Random House.

Delizonna, L. 2017. "High-Performing Teams Need Psychological Safety. Here's How to Create It." *Harvard Business Review*, August 24. https://hbr.org/2017/08/high-performing-teams-need-psychological-safety-heres-how-to-create-it.

Doan, J., and A. Alwan. 2017. "Examining Status Microaggressions and Academic Libraries." *Library Journal*. www.libraryjournal.com/?detailStory=joy-doan-and-ahmed-alwan-examining-status-microaggressions-and-academic-libraries.

Dowd, F. A. 1988. "Latchkey Children in the Library." *Children Today* 17, no. 6: 5–8.

Edmondson, A. 2018. *The Fearless Organization: Creating Psychological Safety in the Workplace for Learning, Innovation, and Growth*. New York: Wiley.

Epstein, M. 2013. "The Trauma of Being Alive." *New York Times*, August 4. www.nytimes.com/2013/08/04/opinion/sunday/the-trauma-of-being-alive.html.

Ettarh, F. 2018. "Vocational Awe and Librarianship: The Lies We Tell Ourselves." In *The Library With the Lead Pipe*, January 10. www.inthelibrarywiththeleadpipe.org/2018/vocational-awe/.

Farmer, A. 2018. "Archiving While Black." *Black Perspectives*. www.aaihs.org/archiving-while-black/.

Feagin, J., H. Vera, and N. Imain. 1996. *Agony of Education: Black Students at a White University*. New York: Routledge.

Ferrell, S. 2010. "Who Says There's a Problem?" *Reference & User Services Quarterly* 50, no. 2: 141–51. https://doi.org/10.5860/rusq.50n2.141.

Fifarek, A. 2014. "Thriving in the New Normal: Strategies for Managing the Scarcity Mindset." *Journal of Library Leadership & Management* 29, no. 1: 1–12.

Flocos, S. 2014. "Sensory Experience and the Workplace." Work Design Magazine. https://workdesign.com/2014/06/sensory-experience-workplace/.

Ford, J. D., J. Chapman, D. F. Connor, and K. R. Cruise. 2012. "Complex Trauma and Aggression in Secure Juvenile Justice Settings." *Criminal Justice and Behavior* 39, no. 6: 694–724. https://doi.org/10.1177/0093854812436957.

Foster, H., and J. Hagan. 2015. "Punishment Regimes and the Multilevel Effects of Parental Incarceration: Intergenerational, Intersectional, and Interinstitutional Models of Social Inequality and Exclusion." *Review of Sociology* 41: 135–58.

Fox, M. J. 2014. "Enabling Gender-Inclusivity in LIS Education through Epistemology, Ethics, and Essential Questions." *Journal of Education for Library and Information Science* 55, no. 3: 241–50.

Franklin, J. H. 2012. "Dilemma of the American Negro." *Black Scholar* 42, no. 1: 17–23.

Freeze, C. n.d. "How Childhood Trauma Can Result in Workplace Violence." https://mrchrisfreeze.com/workplace-violence/.

Freire, P. 1968. *Pedagogy of the Oppressed*. New York: Herder and Herder.

Friedman, M. J. n.d. "PTSD History and Overview." www.ptsd.va.gov/professional/treat/essentials/history_ptsd.asp.

Gallup/Knight Foundation. 2018. "American Views: Trust, Media, and Democracy." https://kf-site-production.s3.amazonaws.com/publications/pdfs/000/000/242/original/KnightFoundation_AmericansViews_Client_Report_010917_Final_Updated.pdf.

Glaze, L. E., and L. M. Maruschak. 2008. "Parents in Prison and Their Minor Children." U.S. Department of Justice, Office of Justice Programs, Bureau of Justice Statistics. Special Report, August 8, 2008.

Gottlieb, A. 2016. "Household Incarceration in Early Adolescence and Risk of Premarital First Birth." *Child Youth Services Review* 61: 126–34.

Greenwald, R. 2005. *Child Trauma Handbook: A Guide for Helping Trauma-Exposed Children and Adolescents*. Binghamton, NY: Haworth Maltreatment and Trauma Press/Haworth Press. https://psycnet.apa.org/record/2005-15293-000.

Harris, M., and R. D. Fallot. 2001. "Envisioning a Trauma-Informed Service System: A Vital Paradigm Shift." *New Directions for Mental Health Services* 89: 3–22. www.ncbi.nlm.nih.gov/pubmed/11291260.

Hedemark, A., and J. Lindberg. 2018. "Babies, Bodies, and Books—Librarians' Work for Early Literacy." *Library Trends* 66, no. 4: 422–41.

Herway, J. 2017. "How to Create a Culture of Psychological Safety." Gallup, December 7. www.gallup.com/workplace/236198/create-culture-psychological-safety.aspx.

Hill, H. 2013. "Disability and Accessibility in the Library and Information Science Literature: A Content Analysis." *Library & Information Science Research* 35, no. 2: 137–42.

Holt-Lunstad, J., T. Smith, M. Baker, T. Harris, and D. Stephenson. 2015. "Loneliness and Social Isolation as Risk Factors for Mortality: A Meta-Analytic Review." *Perspectives on Psychological Science* 10, no. 2: 227–37. doi: 10.1177/1745691614568352.

Ingraham, D. 2017. "Trump Says Sanctuary Cities Are Hotbeds of Crime. Data Says the Opposite." *Washington Post*, January 27. www.washingtonpost.com/news/wonk/wp/2017/01/27/trump-says-sanctuary-cities-are-hotbeds-of-crime-data-say-the-opposite.

Johns Hopkins Medicine. 2019. "Multiple Chemical Sensitivity." www.hopkinsmedicine.org/health/conditions-and-diseases/multiple-chemical-sensitivity.

Jordan, M. W. 2005. "What Is Your Library's Friendliness Factor?" *Public Library Quarterly* 24, no. 4: 81–99. https://doi.org/10.1300/J118v24n04_05.

Keer, G., and A. Carlos. 2015. "The Stereotype Stereotype: Our Obsession with Librarian Representation." *American Libraries,* October 30. https://americanlibrariesmagazine.org/2015/10/30/the-stereotype-stereotype/.

Ko, S. J., J. D. Ford, N. Kassam-Adams, S. J. Berkowitz, C. Wilson, M. Wong, . . . and C. M. Layne. 2008. "Creating Trauma-Informed Systems: Child Welfare, Education, First Responders, Health Care, Juvenile Justice." *Professional Psychology: Research and Practice* 39, no. 4: 396–404. https://doi.org/10.1037/0735-7028.39.4.396.

Kolk, B. A. van der. 2005. "Developmental Trauma Disorder: Toward a Rational Diagnosis for Children with Complex Trauma Histories." *Psychiatric Annals* 35, no. 5: 401–8. https://doi.org/10.3928/00485713-20050501-06.

Kwan, L. B. 2019. "The Collaboration Blind Spot." *Harvard Business Review*, March–April. https://hbr.org/2019/03/the-collaboration-blind-spot.

Lambert, S. L. 2004. "The Library as a Sanctuary for Inner-City Youth: Protections, Implications, Cohesions, Tensions, Recommendations, and Inspirations." Unpublished master's thesis, University of North Carolina, Chapel Hill.

Lepore, J. 2018. "The Academy Is Largely Itself Responsible for Its Own Peril." *Chronicle of Higher Education,* November 13. www.chronicle.com/article/The-Academy-Is-Largely/245080.

Lipsky, L. 2018. *The Age of Overwhelm*. Oakland, CA: Berrett-Koehler.

Lloyd, A. 2009. "Informing Practice: Information Experiences of Ambulance Officers in Training and On-Road Practice." *Journal of Documentation* 65, no. 3: 396–419.

Lopez, G. 2020. "11 Questions about the Coronavirus We Still Can't Answer." Vox, May 12. www.vox.com/2020/5/12/21248395/coronavirus-pandemic-covid-symptoms-testing-children-mysteries.

Lorde, A. 1984. "Age, Race, Class, and Sex: Women Redefining Difference." In *Sister Outsider: Essays and Speeches*. California: Crossing.

Mathieu, F. 2012. *Compassion Fatigue Workbook: Creative Tools for Transforming Compassion Fatigue and Vicarious Traumatization*. Abingdon-on-Thames, UK: Routledge.

Matteson, M. L., and S. S. Miller. 2014. "What Library Managers Should Know about Emotional Labor." *Public Library Quarterly* 33, no. 2: 95–107. doi: 10.1080/01616846.2014.910720.

McGee, N. 2019. "Advocates Throw the Book at Danville Prison." News-Gazette.com, June 9. www.news-gazette.com/news/local/2019-06-09/advocates-throw-the -book-danville-prison.html.

Melilli, A., R. Mitola, and A. Hunsaker. 2016. "Contributing to the Library Student Employee Experience: Perceptions of a Student Development Program." *Journal of Academic Librarianship* 42, no. 4: 430–37. http://dx.doi.org/10.1016/ j.acalib.2016.04.005.

Millsap, K. 2018. "Building Partnerships with Correctional Libraries." *Texas Library Journal* fall: 79–80.

Mogilevsky, M. 2017. "7 Questions to Help You Balance Self-Care and Resistance." Everyday Feminism, February 12. https://everydayfeminism.com/2017/02/ balance-self-care-and-resistance/.

Moniz, R., J. Eshleman, J. Henry, H. Slutzky, and L. Moniz. 2016. *The Mindful Librarian: Connecting the Practice of Mindfulness to Librarianship*. Waltham, MA: Chandos.

Morris, M., M. Conteh, and M. Harris-Perry. 2016. *Pushout: The Criminalization of Black Girls in Schools*. New York: New Press.

Murray, J., D. Farrington, and I. Sekol. 2012. "Children's Antisocial Behavior, Mental Health, Drug Use, and Educational Performance after Parental Incarceration: A Systematic Review and Meta-Analysis." *Psychological Bulletin* 138, no. 2: 175–210.

Murray, L. 2010. *Breaking Night: A Memoir of Forgiveness, Survival, and My Journey from Homeless to Harvard*. New York: Hachette Books.

National Library of Medicine. 2010. "Psychosomatic Medicine: The Puzzling Leap." www.nlm.nih.gov/hmd/emotions/psychosomatic.html.

Pollard, H. B., C. Shivakumar, J. Starr, O. Eidelman, D. M. Jacobowitz, C. L. Dalgard, and R. J. Ursano. 2016. "'Soldier's Heart': A Genetic Basis for Elevated Cardiovascular Disease Risk Associated with Post-Traumatic Stress Disorder." *Frontiers in Molecular Neuroscience* 9. https://doi.org/10.3389/ fnmol.2016.00087.

Provence, M. A. 2019. "From Nuisances to Neighbors." *Advances in Social Work* 18, no. 4: 1053–67. https://doi.org/10.18060/22321.

Reale, M. 2017. *Becoming a Reflective Librarian and Teacher: Strategies for Mindful Academic Practice*. Chicago: American Library Association.

Redford, R., director. 2015. *Paper Tigers* documentary film.

Richardson, S. A. n.d. "Awareness of Trauma-Informed Care." *Social Work Today*. www .socialworktoday.com/archive/exc_012014.shtml.

Robinson, P. 2016. *You Can't Touch My Hair: And Other Things I Still Have to Explain.* New York: Penguin Random House.

SAMSHA. 2014. "SAMHSA's Concept of Trauma and Guidance for a Trauma-Informed Approach." https://store.samhsa.gov/system/files/sma14-4884.pdf.

Shelton, J., and J. Winkelstein. 2014. "Librarians and Social Workers: Working Together for Homeless LGBTQ Youth." *Young Adult Library Services* 13, no. 1 (fall): 20–24.

Simmons, R. 1985. "The Homeless in the Public Library: Implications for Access to Libraries." *RQ* 25, no. 1: 110–20.

Sloan, K., J. Vanderfluit, and J. Douglas. 2019. "Not 'Just My Problem to Handle': Emerging Themes on Secondary Trauma and Archivists." *Journal of Contemporary Archival Studies* 6, no. 20: 1–24.

Smith, P. S. 2008. "Mildly Delirious Libraries: Transforming Your Library from Top to Bottom." *Journal of Access Services* 5, no. 1–2: 19–30. https://doi .org/10.1080/15367960802197665.

Soska, T. M. 2018. "Innovative Social Work Managers Need to Spend More Time at Their Public Libraries." In *Papers for the Community Collaboration Track Network of Social Work Management Annual Conference*, 1–14. San Diego, CA. https:// socialworkmanager.org/2018-conference-presentations/.

Sun, J., Patel, F., Rose-Jacobs, R., Frank, D.A., Black, M.M. and Chilton, M. 2017. "Mothers' Adverse Childhood Experiences and Their Young Children's Development." *American Journal of Preventative Medicine* 53, no. 6: 882–91.

Tolley, R. 2020. "A Leaf of Faith: Creating Positive, Productive Library Spaces with Plants." In *The Library Workplace Idea Book: Proactive Steps for Positive Change*, 41–48. Chicago: American Library Association.

Turner, C. 2017. "Bodleian Library's Keeper of the Books May Have Died from Asbestos Poisoning, Inquest Told." *The Telegraph*, October 26.

Twenge, J. M. 2017. "Have Smartphones Destroyed a Generation?" *The Atlantic*, September. www.theatlantic.com/magazine/archive/2017/09/has-the-smartphone-destroyed-a-generation/534198/.

University of Denver, Graduate School of Social Work. 2018. "Library Social Work." https://socialwork.du.edu/news/library-social-work.

Varheim, A. 2014. "Trust in Libraries and Trust in Most People: Social Capital Creation in the Public Library." *Library Quarterly: Information, Community, Policy* 84, no. 3: 258–77.

Welteroth, E. 2019. *More Than Enough: Claiming Space for Who You Are No Matter What They Say.* London: Penguin.

Whitmire, E. 2004. "The Campus Racial Climate and Undergraduates' Perceptions of the Academic Library." *portal: Libraries and the Academy* 4, no. 3: 363–78. doi: 10.1353/pla.2004.0057.

Wildeman, C. 2013. "Parental Incarceration, Child Homelessness, and the Invisible Consequences of Mass Imprisonment." *Annals of the American Academy of Political and Social Science* 651, no. 1: 74–96.

Wilkin, L., and S. Hillock. 2014. "Enhancing MSW Students' Efficacy in Working with Trauma, Violence, and Oppression: An Integrated Feminist-Trauma Framework for Social Work Education." *Feminist Teacher* 24, no. 3: 184–206. https://muse .jhu.edu/article/589359.

Wiseman, T. 1996. "A Concept Analysis of Empathy." *Journal of Advanced Nursing* 23: 1162–67. https://pdfs.semanticscholar.org/0cd0/ 2f528a829e286c016230030a9f72f5653921.pdf.

Wolverton, B. C., W. L. Douglas, and K. Bounds. 1989. "A Study of Interior Landscape Plants for Indoor Air Pollution Abatement." https://ntrs.nasa.gov/search .jsp?R=19930072988.

Yohn, D. L. 2019. "Why Every Company Needs a Chief Experience Officer." *Harvard Business Review*, June 13. https://hbr.org/2019/06/why-every-company-needs-a-chief-experience-officer?utm_medium=email&utm_ source=newsletter_daily&utm_campaign=dailyalert_not_ activesubs&referral=00563&deliveryName=DM40181.

Zettervall, S., and M. Nienow. 2019. *Whole Person Librarianship: A Social Work Approach to Patron Services*. Santa Barbara, CA: Libraries Unlimited.

Index

empathy (*cont'd*)
    self-care for, 139
    staff behavior for trauma-informed
      care, 26
    sympathy *vs.*, 22
    trauma-informed framework for
      building, vii
employee assistance programs (EAPs), 77
employee experience (EX), 134–135
empowerment
    choice for, 95
    library program procedures, questions
      about, 119
    of library staff, gender issues and, 102
    of patrons, 89–91
"empty vessel" model, 87
Enoch Pratt Free Library, 129–130
environment
    See space; trauma-informed library
      environment
environmental microaggressions, 107
epistemology, 69, 70
Epstein, Mark, 3
equity, 28
ESFT Model, 98
essential oils, 37, 142
Ettarh, Fobazi, 50, 71
ETSU
    See East Tennessee State University
EX (employee experience), 134–135
externalizing, 11

F

Facebook group, 81
faculty
    at ETSU, 42, 43, 104
    library as sanctuary and, 123–124
    microaggressions towards library
      faculty, 108
    physical safety and, 48
    psychological safety and, 55
failures, 148
"fake news," 70, 71
Fallot, R. D., 22, 116–117
family
    dissolution of family unit, effect on
      children, 9–10
    household challenges, 7–11
    neglect, 11–13

    roles born of trauma, 133–134
    See also parents
Family Educational Rights and Privacy
    Act, 65
Farmer, Ashley, 101
Farrington, D., 10
fathers, 10–11
    See also parents
Feagin, J., 101
*The Fearless Organization: Creating
    Psychological Safety in the Workplace
    for Learning, Innovation, and Growth*
    (Edmondson), 53
Federal Bureau of Investigation (FBI), 129
feedback
    sharing, importance of, 55–56
    for trauma-informed care plan, 146
female friend, 81
feminists, 20
Ferguson (MO) Public Library, 129
Ferguson, Plessy v., 100
Ferrell, S., 23–24
Fifarek, Amy, 62
fines, library, 41
First Amendment, 129
Flocos, S., 41
Forbes.com, 80
forest bathing (*shinrin-yoku*), 143
formal services policy, 119
Foster, H., 10
foster care system, 11
Foucault, Michel, 68
four Rs
    development of, 17
    overview of, 18–19
Fox, Melodie J., 69
fragrances, 37
Franklin, John Hope, 101
free speech, 41–43
Freedom Libraries, 101
Freeze, Christopher, 57
Freire, Paulo, 87
"frequent flyers," 87
Freud, Sigmund, 19
Friendliness Factor, 33
furniture
    interior design of library, 38
    patron choices about, 93
future, vision for, 128

trauma-informed transformation of
library services, 21–23
user-centered libraries, 32–33
voice of patrons and, 91–92
libraries
choice of patrons, 93–95
collaboration in, 83–85
customer service, evaluation of, 33–34
customer service, trauma-informed
approach to, 30–31
empowerment of patrons, 89–91
gender issues and, 102–105
historical issues, 99–102
knowledge, organizing, 69–71
labels, service without, 23–24
Library Code of Ethics, 28–30
microaggressions in, 107–110
moral safety in, 58–60
mutuality in, 85
organizational readiness for change,
assessment of, 113–121
outcomes with trauma-informed care,
24–25
peer support in academic libraries,
75–77
peer support in library organizations,
77–79
physical safety of, 47–50
planning for trauma-informed services,
145–150
psychological safety of patrons, 51–53
public trust, 71–72
safe spaces for trauma survivors, 21
social safety and, 56–58
staff behavior for trauma-informed
care, 25–26
transparency of, 62–63
trauma-informed care and, 18–19,
27–34
trauma-informed transformation of,
21–23
trustworthiness/transparency and,
61–62
user-centered, switch to, 32–33
voice of patrons, 91–92
library administration
See administrators

library anxiety, 61
library as sanctuary
library as places of sanctuary in
sanctuary cities, 129–130
professional literature on, 124–126
Sanctuary Model, 126–128
school library as sanctuary, 123–124
Library Bill of Rights (American Library
Association), 26
library board members, 90
Library Code of Ethics (American Library
Association)
moral safety and, 59
principals of, 28–30
trauma-informed care and, 27
trust in librarians and, 71
library environment, trauma-informed
building maintenance, 40
children, special considerations for, 41
free speech, conflict in, 41–43
indoor air quality, 37–39
interior design, 37
neutral spaces, 40–41
at Palm Beach Public Library, 35–36
senses, examination of library with,
36–38
library fines, 41
library organizations, 77–79
library procedures
empowerment of patrons and, 90–91
readiness for change, assessment of,
117–119
transparency for public trust, 72
transparency of, 62
library workers
choice of patrons and, 93–95
collaboration/mutuality and, 83–88
cultural issues and, 98–99
customer service, evaluation of, 33–34
customer service, trauma-informed
approach to, 30–31
emotional labor of, 132–133
employee experience, 134–135
empowerment of, 90–91
gender issues and, 102–105
as helpers, 131
historical issues, 99–102

social safety and, 57–58
power differential
  minimizing, 52
  traumatic experience and, 18
practical trust, 64
preachers, 42–43
prison libraries, 126
privacy
  choices about, 94–95
  formal services policy on, 119
  library as sanctuary and, 129
  of library patrons, 25
  "Vegas" rule for, 138
"problem patron"
  behavior, ingrained beliefs about, 30–31
  labeling of, 23–24
  as negative terminology, 29
  problem with term, 87
  voice of, 91
procedures
  See library procedures
professional development
  on microaggressions, 109
  peer support in library organizations, 77
  for trauma-informed care, 30
  warmth training for reference desk, 147
Provence, M. A., 24
psychological safety
  of library workers, 53–56
  of patrons, 51–53
psychological trauma, 3–4
PTSD
  See post-traumatic stress disorder
public libraries
  historical issues, 99–102
  public trust in, 71–72
  as sanctuary, 124–126, 129–130
public trust, 71–72
Purvis, Robert, 100
Pushout: The Criminalization of Black Girls in Schools (Morris, Conteh, & Harris-Perry), 75–76

Q

Questionnaire, Adverse Childhood Experience, 151–153

questions
  about cultural, historical, gender issues, 97–98
  about cultural issues, 98
  about historical issues, 100
  about microaggressions, 109
  about social safety, 57–58
  about trust, 66–67
  for assessment of organizational readiness for change, 114–115, 117–121
  for evaluation of psychological safety of library workers, 53–54
  for peer support needs analysis, 78
  for psychological safety, 56
  for self-assessment, 115

R

race/ethnicity
  cultural issues for library service, 98–99
  historical issues, 100–102
  historical trauma and, 105–107
  microaggressions and, 107–110
  parental incarceration and, 10, 11
"Racial Microaggressions in Academic Libraries: Results of a Survey of Minority and Non-Minority Librarians" (Alabi), 107–108
racism
  historical issues for libraries and, 100–102
  historical trauma and, 106, 107
  microaggressions and, 107–110
readiness surveys/questionnaires, 116
Reale, Michelle, 139
realization, 18–19
Reboot: Leadership and the Art of Growing Up (Colonna), 57
recognition, 18–19
Reconstruction, 100
red flag, 104
Reference and User Services Association (RUSA), 30
reference interview, 85
reference service
  service policy of, 31
  warmth training, 147
regulars, 86–87

Substance Abuse and Mental Health
Services Administration
(SAMHSA), 17, 18
Sun, J., 15
support
See peer support
survey
for peer support needs analysis, 78
readiness surveys, 116
sustainability, 39
sympathy
empathy *vs.*, 22
library as sanctuary and, 124
symptoms
micro habits of self-care and, 140
of traumatic stress, 19–20

T
taste, 37
"Team Learning and Psychological Safety
Survey" (Edmondson), 53
teams
collaboration in libraries, 83–85
safe team environment, 136
"techno-chauvinism," 63
teen advisory groups, 72, 74
teen volunteers, 74
teenagers
See adolescents
therapy animals, 38
three Es, 17, 18
three pillars, of trauma-informed care, 21
360-degree feedback model, 56
TIC
See trauma-informed care
timeline, for trauma-informed care plan,
147
tobacco smoke, 38, 40
Tolley, Rebecca, 125
touching, 138
toxic stress, 128
toxic workplaces, 135–137
toxicity, antidotes to, 137–139
training
for cultural humility, 99
of library staff, yearly, 149–150
safety training for library staff, 49

staff training about trauma-informed
practices, 114
staff training/education, assessment
of, 120
of teen volunteers, 74
warmth training, 147, 149
transparency
honesty/discretion for, 65–66
library program procedures, questions
about, 118
organizational culture and, 63–65
for public trust, 72
of trauma-informed libraries, 62–63
trust and, 61–62
trauma
abuse, 6–7
ACEs score, 14–15
adverse childhood experiences, 4–6
definition of, 3–4
emotional labor of library workers and,
132–133
four Rs of trauma-informed care,
18–19
historical trauma, 105–107
household challenges, 7–11
library workers and, 131–132
neglect, 11–13
roles born of, 133–134
three Es of trauma-informed care, 18
use of term, ix
trauma champions, 145–146
trauma theory
research requests about, vii–viii
as Sanctuary Model pillar, 128
trauma-informed care (TIC)
collaboration/mutuality, 83–88
cultural, historical, gender issues,
97–110
customer service, evaluation of, 33–34
customer service in libraries, 30–31
empowerment/voice/choice, 89–95
four Rs, 18–19
libraries and, 27–34
library as sanctuary, 123–130
Library Code of Ethics and, 28–30
organizational readiness for,
assessment of, 113–121